W9-BLH-589

Carl Sandburg

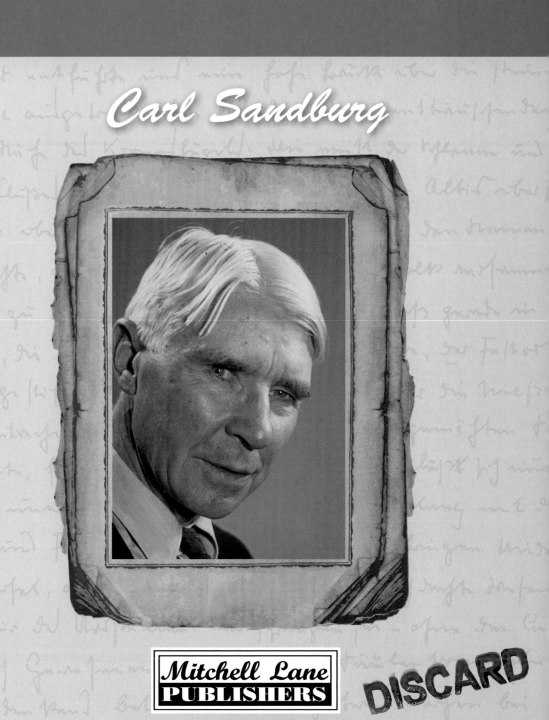

Mitchell Lane
PUBLISHERS

P.O. Box 196
Hockessin, Delaware 19707

Poets and Playwrights

Carl Sandburg

Emily Dickinson

Langston Hughes

Tennessee Williams

William Shakespeare

Carl Sandburg

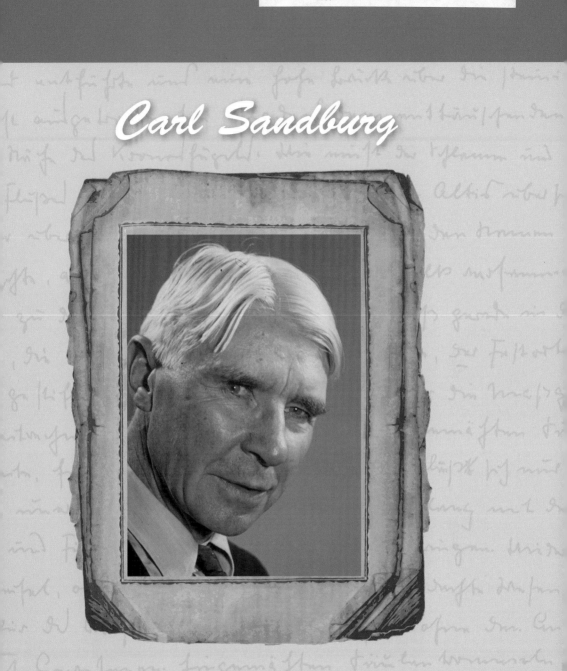

Rebecca Thatcher Murcia

Printing   1   2   3   4   5   6   7   8   9

Library of Congress Cataloging-in-Publication Data
Murcia, Rebecca Thatcher, 1962–
    Carl Sandburg/by Rebecca Thatcher Murcia.
        p. cm. — (Poets and playwrights)
    Includes bibliographical references and index.
    ISBN 1-58415-430-6 (library bound: alk. paper)
    1. Sandburg, Carl, 1878–1967—Juvenile literature. 2. Poets, American—United States—Biography—Juvenile literature. I. Title. II. Series.
    PS3537.A618Z783
    811'.52—dc22
                                                                            2005028504
    ISBN-13: 9781584154303

ABOUT THE AUTHOR: Rebecca Thatcher Murcia graduated from the University of Massachusetts at Amherst and worked as a newspaper reporter for fifteen years. She lives with her two sons in Akron, Pennsylvania. Among her other books for Mitchell Lane Publishers are *The Civil Rights Movement* and *E.B. White.*

PHOTO CREDITS: Cover, pp. 1, 3—Eric Schaal/Time Life Pictures/Getty Images; pp. 12, 22, 27, 35, 42—Library of Congress; p. 32—MPI/Getty Images; pp. 42, 72—Allan Grant/Time Life Pictures/Getty Images; p. 50—John Whiting/Pix Inc./Time Life Pictures/Getty Images; p. 62—Slim Aarons/Getty Images; p. 82—Paul Schutzer/Time Life Pictures/Getty Images; p. 92—Evans/Three Lions/Getty Images.

PUBLISHER'S NOTE: This story is based on the author's extensive research, which she believes to be accurate. Documentation of such research is contained on pages 108–109.

    The internet sites referenced herein were active as of the publication date. Due to the fleeting nature of some web sites, we cannot guarantee they will all be active when you are reading this book.

                                                                            PLB

Contents

*For Your Information

Chicago remains a gleaming metropolis—with a gritty underbelly—more than ninety years after Carl Sandburg called it *The City of Big Shoulders* in his award-winning poem. Sandburg loved the city even though he was intimately familiar with its dark side. A book of the young Sandburg's journalism on the Chicago Race Riots of 1919 was republished fifty years later, a rare honor for a reporter's collected articles.

Chapter
1

A Shock in Chicago

Carl Sandburg walked up the steps to the office of *Poetry* magazine late in the day in the fall of 1914. He was a child of immigrants, a former hobo turned hardworking newspaper reporter who also wrote poetry. A few months earlier, the magazine had published his new poem, simply titled "Chicago." The poem was brutally honest about Chicago in the early twentieth century. It described the way the city was full of energy but also full of violence and hunger. Its opening lines are famous:

Hog Butcher for the World,
Tool Maker, Stacker of Wheat,
Player with Railroads and the Nation's Freight Handler;
Stormy, husky, brawling,
City of Big Shoulders

The poem goes on to say that the negative way people described Chicago is often true. "They tell me you are wicked and I believe them, for I have seen your painted women under the gas lamps luring the farm boys. / And they tell me you are crooked and I answer: Yes, it is true I have seen the gunman kill and go free to kill again."

After Sandburg allowed that what the critics said about Chicago was true, he described what he saw as beautiful about the city. "Fierce as a dog with tongue lapping for action, cunning as a savage pitted against the wilderness, / Bareheaded, / Shoveling, / Wrecking, / Planning, / Building, breaking, rebuilding." The poem concludes by going back to what Sandburg had said about Chicago at the beginning: "Hog Butcher, Tool Maker, Stacker of Wheat, Player with Railroads and Freight Handler to the Nation."[1]

The unusual poem, which broke clearly with typical poetic style of the time, caused a lot of controversy when *Poetry* published it. Some were shocked that Sandburg would use everyday language, or even slang, in poetry. Poetry was supposed to be elegant and fancy and Sandburg's was not. One magazine, *The Dial*, said the work did not even deserve to be categorized as poetry. Others liked Sandburg's style and his understanding of the city of Chicago. Almost 100 years later, many Chicago residents still view fondly the way Sandburg called their urban outpost the "City of Big Shoulders." Harriet Monroe, the editor of *Poetry* magazine, wrote soon after "Chicago" was published that she was proud her magazine took chances on groundbreaking poetry like Sandburg's. "We have taken chances, made room for the young and the new, tried to break the chains which enslave Chicago to New York, America to Europe, and the present to the past."[2]

When Sandburg walked up the steps on that chilly fall day, he only expected to visit with his friends at the office. One of the magazine workers, a poet named Eunice Tietjens, handed him the November issue, trying to hide her excitement about the secret inside.

Sandburg opened the magazine and there was the incredible news. "Chicago," with all its frank imagery and brutal phrases, had been awarded the $200 Levinson Prize as the best American poem of 1914. Sandburg, the controversial, struggling poet, had received national recognition for a controversial poem that was truly about Chicago's struggle.

The board of directors of *Poetry* magazine had found it difficult to decide whether to give the award to Sandburg. Poetry experts, especially the famous Ezra Pound in England, had suggested other poems. In 1914, the concept of free verse—poetry that was not in a set number of syllables per line, or with a rhyming word at the end of every line—was still a fairly new idea. Some poets were openly critical of Sandburg's free verse style; famous American poet Robert Frost said writing free verse was like playing tennis with the net down. One of the board members suggested they look for a dictionary. They found one, and it said that poetry was "the art which has for its object the exciting of intellectual pleasure by means of vivid, imaginative, passionate and inspiring language, usually though not necessarily arranged in the form of measured verse or numbers."[3] Hobart C. Chatfield-Taylor, a novelist and wealthy man who supported the magazine, was usually very traditional. Chatfield-Taylor said he liked Sandburg's poem more than any of the other nominated poems.

Not only was Sandburg thrilled to be recognized for the poem, but the $200 was also a major bonus in 1914. Sandburg cracked that the money would "octuple"—or multiply by eight—the bank account he shared with his wife, Lilian, whom he called Paula. He asked Tietjens to take a walk with him. As they walked, he spoke about the prize and then dropped it and talked about something else. Then he spoke of it again and dropped it again. Tietjens realized how thoroughly shocked Sandburg was by the award. "At last I saw that the shock of pleasure had been so great that he could not think of it at once, as one cannot put one's hand on a hot stove and leave it there. Only after the news had cooled a little in his heart could he settle down hard on it."[4]

The Levinson Prize was a fantastic success for the thirty-six-year-old poet, but the success had not come easily. Sandburg had worked for years on his writing and had persevered despite all the rejections and all the hard work that was involved. He had wanted to write since he was a child.

Poetry Magazine

In the early 1900s, people did not have to look hard to find poetry. Poetry was published in newspapers and magazines. The best poets were well known, and even regarded as celebrities. Still, at a time when artists like Pablo Picasso were creating a new, different kind of modern art and musicians were experimenting with new rhythms and instruments, much of American poetry seemed to be stuck in the 1800s. The poetry commonly printed in newspapers and magazines was not bad, but it tended to follow strict rhyming patterns that had been established long before in England. The themes, such as love or the weather, were sometimes overused or corny.

Chicago poet Harriet Monroe wanted to encourage other poets to expand their boundaries and explore new forms. She began a magazine that supported poets by paying them for their work, and encouraged them to break the tired mold of a strictly rhyming poem with a certain amount of syllables in each line. Her goal was also that the magazine's offices be a place where poets could gather to socialize and talk about their work. "The Open Door will be the policy of this magazine—may the great poet we are looking for never find it shut, or half-shut, against his ample genius!" Monroe wrote at the magazine's founding in 1912.[5]

Monroe had lofty goals. She wanted to change the way American poetry was written, presented, and published. She had no personal fortune to use toward her big dream, but she knew people who were wealthy. She went to work raising money, finding subscribers, and finding poems to publish. Ezra Pound, an American poet who was living in England, was enthusiastic and supportive. Monroe named him the magazine's foreign correspondent. She printed two of his poems in the first issue, "Middle-Aged" and "To Whistler, American." In "To Whistler, American," Pound used artist James Abbott McNeill Whistler's exhibit in England to muse about the struggle to turn the American "impulse into art." He concluded that there was hope for art in America, noting, "You and Abe Lincoln from that mass of dolts / Show us there's chance at least of winning through."[6]

Although many of the poems broke with established norms and created new styles, some were just good, simple poems. Joyce Kilmer's "Trees," which ends with the lines, "Poems were made by fools like me / But only God can make a tree,"[7] was one of the most popular poems the magazine published.

Although the magazine would struggle financially for many years, it was almost immediately successful in presenting new poetry and

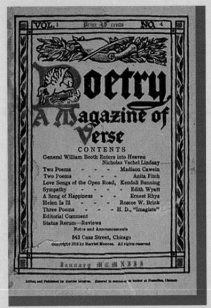

One of *Poetry* magazine's first covers

new poets. In 1915 *Poetry* published T.S. Elliot's "The Love Song of J. Alfred Prufock," a strange, first-person account of an aging man fulminating on his not very satisfying love life. It was a landmark for *Poetry* magazine and for Elliot, who was not a well-known poet at the time but would go on to become one of the most important poets of the twentieth century. The magazine would also publish important work by such poets as William Carlos Williams, Robert Frost, and, of course, Carl Sandburg. When Monroe died in 1936, Sandburg said her magazine had helped begin a "period that would see more widespread, furious and reckless adventure and experimenting across twenty years than had been known in two hundred years before."[8]

Even though the magazine was important to poets, it was not a very successful business. Frequently the editors were afraid they would have to close the magazine because they did not make much money from advertising or subscription sales. They always tried to be kind and friendly, even when they thought a poet's work was not good enough to publish. This custom ultimately insured the magazine's long-term financial stability.

Ruth Lilly, a multimillionaire whose family founded Ely Lilly and Company pharmaceuticals, submitted poems to the magazine in 1972. The editors did not publish the poems, but they wrote her nice notes declining to purchase them. Lilly liked the way they treated her and offered to sponsor a poetry prize, a $100,000 award for lifetime achievement, in 1986. In 2001, she gave the magazine $100 million, among the largest gifts ever made to a magazine in American history.

The magazine editors used the money to form a foundation that would promote reading, writing, and reciting poetry throughout the United States. They plan to continue, of course, to keep the door open to any poet's "ample genius."

People from Sweden left their homeland in large numbers throughout the 1800s and early 1900s. In this picture, they are embarking from Goteburg, Sweden, for England and America in 1905. Sandburg's parents made a similar voyage in the previous century. August Sandburg sailed to the United States in 1869 and Clara Andersdatter, who would later become his wife, traveled in 1873.

Chapter 2

A Child of Immigrants

The man who would become one of America's best-loved poets was born in humble surroundings. Carl's parents, August and Clara Sandburg, fled poverty and the threat of war in Sweden to make new lives for themselves in the United States. Ordinary working people, they crossed the Atlantic Ocean in "steerage," or the least expensive area of the great transatlantic sailing ships that brought thousands of immigrants from Europe to the New World during the 1800s. The Sandburgs moved to Galesburg, Illinois, after August Sandburg heard there was work on the railroad in that state. Galesburg, founded in 1834, was surrounded by prairie and farmland. Although it was small, it did have some bragging rights. Christian missionaries founded Knox College there in 1837. Lombard College was established in 1853. Abraham Lincoln and Stephen A. Douglas, both candidates for the U.S. Senate from Illinois, held one of their famous 1858 debates in Galesburg.

Carl was born at home on January 6, 1878. The Sandburgs already had a three-year-old daughter, Mary. Soon more boys, Martin, Emil, and Fred, and two more sisters, Esther and Martha, were born. Carl's father worked long hours as a blacksmith's assistant for the local railroad, but he had very little education and never earned high wages. The family had enough food to eat, but there was no money for any luxuries. For Christmas,

August Sandburg would usually give each child a bag of candy, an orange, and a small toy such as a pocketknife.

The Sandburgs spoke a rudimentary form of English, but they preferred their native language, Swedish. Carl and his brothers and sisters all learned Swedish from their parents. The family liked to visit Clara Sandburg's cousin, Lena Krans, at her farm out in the country. Carl enjoyed the long carriage rides to the farm. One day when he was about three, his parents went inside the farmhouse to visit. Carl climbed up into the carriage, grabbed the reins, and was about to go for a drive. "Oh Glory! I was going to call 'Giddap,' to the horses," he wrote later.[1] The adults noticed and came running outside to haul Carl down from the wagon and scold him.

The next year Carl, who called himself Charlie as a boy, noticed his family owned a Swedish Bible. He asked his mother to show it to him and explain how reading worked. He did not quite understand his mother's explanation, but he did get the idea that there was something great about the written word. Carl's mother told him he would understand it better when he went to school.

At about the age of seven, Carl went to a neighborhood school. This was before kindergarten and preschool were common. He was thrilled when his first teacher, Miss Ward, taught him the basics of reading and writing. He was usually a good student, but once in second grade he wrote a note to a friend in his class with some swear words in it. He had to stay after school and write: "Trifles make perfection and perfection is no trifle" 200 times on the blackboard.[2]

At home, Carl and his brothers did the many chores that were normal for children in the 1800s. They had to keep the house warm in the winter by going out to the coal bin, breaking up the big lumps with a hammer, and bringing the coal into the house to burn in the stove. The coal stove kept the kitchen warm, but no heat made its way to the little third-floor room where Carl and Martin slept. They would run up the stairs at night and try to get under the covers before the cold air chilled them in their light underclothes. The children were also responsible for keeping the house supplied with water from an outdoor pump. Once he earned a spanking from his father when he ignored his father's request for help in the garden.

Carl was told to pick potato bugs off his family's potato plants but instead played in a nearby pasture all day.

Carl was only seven when Ulysses S. Grant, the great Civil War general, died in 1885. Grant had led the Union forces to victory during the Civil War and was elected president in 1868. The Sandburgs attended a parade in Grant's honor when the beloved general died. Carl later remembered that he understood little of Grant's importance at the time, but he could tell that the man's death meant something to his immigrant parents as well as to the many Galesburg residents who had witnessed or fought in the Civil War just a few decades earlier.

As Carl grew older, he immersed himself in any history book he could find. Some of them, such as a book about the American Revolution called *The Boys of '76*, he read over and over again. He also paid close attention to the local and national news. Railroad engineers went on strike in Galesburg in 1888, protesting their low pay and long hours. The conflict between the workers and the owners of the railroad escalated. A detective hired by the railroad owners shot one of the engineers. Without knowing very much about the details of the conflict, Carl was viscerally, passionately, on the side of the strikers. "I was a partisan. I could see only one side to the dispute though my little head did not think and had no accurate information about what lay behind the crying and the shooting," Carl remembered.[3]

Carl, his brother Martin, and a few friends walked the four and a half miles to the county fair in Knoxville every year, eager to take in all the excitement of the competitions and exhibitions. They walked because they wanted to save their money. Admission to the fair was twenty-five cents, and there were certain experiences on which they knew they wanted to spend money. The most important was the Edison Talking Phonograph booth. The telegraph had been invented by this time, but there were still no telephones, radios, or stereos, so the newly invented phonograph, an early type of record player, was a novelty. For five cents, fairgoers could strap on earphones and listen to a voice describing the invention and then hear the recording of a brass band. Years later, Carl remembered, "We stepped up with our nickels. We plugged our ears with the phone ends. We watched the cylinder on the machine turning. . . . We looked at each other's faces

Thomas Edison's phonograph

and nodded and smiled, 'It works! I can hear it! Ain't it the doggonedest thinga-majig? I wouldn't believe it if I wasn't hearing it.' "[4]

When the circus came to town, the boys would show up early in the morning and try to get jobs helping set up the circus and taking care of the animals. If they were lucky, they earned tickets to the show. If they were not chosen to work at the circus and they did not have money for admission, they would try to sneak into the tent when the attendants weren't looking. Once Carl had almost managed to get all the way inside the tent when an attendant grabbed him by the ankles, pulled him out, and told him to go away.

In church, Carl was usually like most children, sitting quietly in the pew, not really paying attention to what was being said but not really ignoring the sermon either. One Sunday, the pastor of the Swedish Lutheran Church gave such a dynamic sermon on Judgment Day that Carl and everybody else in the church paid close attention. The pastor, Carl A. Beckman, said that on Judgment Day, friends would be torn away from friends and children taken away from parents. God would take the good people with him to heaven and the sinners would be forever damned. The message was delivered so forcefully and the torment of the separated loved ones was so well portrayed that Carl remembered that the entire congregation appeared to be traumatized. "I have no memory of a congregation after a sermon walking out with such sober and subdued faces, with such searching looks into each other's faces," he wrote later.[5]

After church, the family went home and gathered around the table to eat fried chicken, mashed potatoes, pickles, and a Swedish dish made from dried fruit. A guest, a delegate to a meeting of Lutherans, ate with the family. The conversation turned to the topic of the day's sermon. The family remembered the graphic way the pastor had said that on Judgment Day, God would decide to send some people to the fires of hell for all eternity while others would go to heaven, and that there was no way to know who would be sent where. Suddenly everyone at the table was crying. Carl was shocked because he had never before seen his father cry. "Down our cheeks the tears ran and we looked at each other," Carl wrote later. "In unison we wept. Slowly we gulped and choked down the sorrow that had come suddenly, the sorrow that arose out of the mystery of what the judgment will be on us in the Last Day."[6]

When Carl was eleven years old, he started working at two jobs. In the mornings before school, he cleaned a real estate office. First he swept the floor. Then he took the office's two spittoons—large metal bowls into which tobacco chewers and smokers would spit—and cleaned them carefully. The work took less than half an hour and paid twenty-five cents a week. After school, Carl and the other newspaper carriers hurried to the offices of the Galesburg *Republican-Register*. Carl picked up between fifty and sixty papers and delivered them to subscribers on three nearby streets. It took about an hour. He earned a dollar a week, plus an extra paper every day that he could take home and read. From the paper, he learned that some of his customers were important. One was Clark E. Carr, who had worked for the governor of Illinois during the Civil War and helped plan the ceremonies dedicating the Gettysburg cemetery. It was at those ceremonies that Abraham Lincoln delivered the unforgettable Gettysburg address, in which he so famously thanked the fallen soldiers for their dedication and called on all Americans to rededicate themselves to the cause for which the soldiers had given their lives: "That the nation shall, under God, have a new birth of freedom, and that government of the people, by the people, for the people shall not perish from the earth."[7]

Earning twenty-five cents for sweeping offices and cleaning spit, and a dollar for delivering newspapers all week, may seem like very low wages today, and indeed, it was not a lot of money for the amount of time Carl spent at his work. But prices were much lower in the 1890s than they are today. At the end of the week, Carl could splurge on an egg sandwich at the local lunch counter for five cents. He and his fellow newsboys would feel like grown-ups, earning money and spending it on a restaurant meal.

Later Carl picked up more newspaper routes. He began delivering the Chicago papers in the morning and learned the importance of delivering the right newspaper to the right person. *The Chicago Times* was allied with the Democratic Party and the *Chicago Tribune* was the Republican paper. A subscriber who was expecting the *Chicago Tribune*, and its Republican slant on the news, would be likely to swear at Carl if he received the *Times*, with its Democratic bias.

Sometimes when Carl had time to sit down and read the papers, he would puzzle over the debates of the day. Politicians were arguing about whether there should be a tariff, or tax, on tin and wool. Some said the tariffs would be good for American workers and others said workers would suffer with the tariffs. Carl read the articles and wondered if the debates just gave the politicians something to argue about. "I began to doubt whether there were tariffs on tin and wool," he wrote. "It was some kind of excitement of arguing to see if anyone would run out of arguments."[8]

It was not only the newspapers that prompted young Carl to begin thinking and wondering about the wider world. New neighbors, the Sjodins, moved in from Chicago. The father was a tailor and a political radical. The son, John Sjodin, was about two years older than Carl. The two boys would sit outside on the grass on summer evenings and talk about politics and economics. The Sjodins believed that the government should do more to help the poor. They were angry about the rich having more money than they knew what to do with and the poor not knowing where they would get their next meal. John Sjodin would laugh about how capitalists wanted the government to leave business alone, but they happily accepted free land from the government to build railroads. The Sjodins dreamed of a future revolution, in which working people would take over the government and make sure the government worked for the benefit of the poor. On the other hand, John Sjodin was a gentle person who always impressed Carl with his lack of hatred and his willingness to try to understand people. "He would argue his points with anybody but he wouldn't let an argument or a debate run into a quarrel. He had his own reverence for life and said many a time that he couldn't hate a millionaire and most of the rich were sorry fools," Carl wrote later.[9] "He made me know I ought to know more about what was going on in politics, industry, business, and crime over the widespread American scene."[10]

And over the widespread American scene in the early 1890s, the economy was going into the worst financial crisis in American history. Railroads went into bankruptcy, companies failed, and workers lost their jobs in what became known as the Panic of 1893. Carl's father, August, who had always worked long days at the railroad, began coming home at noon because the economic crisis had forced the owners of the railroad to shorten workers' hours.

In June of 1892, Carl was fourteen and had finished eighth grade. Today, it would be shocking and even illegal under our mandatory schooling laws for a child to leave school at that age. But in the 1890s, the laws and expectations were different, and times were hard: Carl's family needed money. The bright student wanted to keep studying, but instead he went to work full-time. School was a dream he would postpone for many years.

The American Railroad

In the modern world of jet planes and the Internet, it is hard to imagine how important the railroad was in the nineteenth century. Carl Sandburg, like children throughout the United States in that era, witnessed the way America developed as her railroads grew.

Throughout the 1800s, as Americans settled the West, the railroads went with them. Towns sprang up when the railroad came in; they withered when the railroad passed them by. Politicians traveled the country in trains, sometimes giving speeches without even getting off their railroad car in what were known as whistle-stop tours. The trains brought traveling theater groups, circus performers, and lecturers, delivering culture, entertainment, and wisdom.

The construction of the great railway routes became a part of American history, folklore, and mythology. People told stories and wrote songs about the building of the railroads and the men who operated the massive locomotives. Great fortunes were made as railroad companies, with land given to them by the government, expanded their networks across the country. Workers who built the railroads, operated the trains, handled the freight, and took care of the passengers formed labor unions and became an important part of the growing American labor movement.

The concept of using rails to move wheeled vehicles traces back to England hundreds of years ago, when miners used carts on rails pulled by horses. Trains, however, did not become a great system of transportation until the steam locomotive was invented in England in the early 1800s. Inventors kept designing bigger and more powerful locomotives throughout the early part of the century. Engineers also had to figure out how the powerful engines would be stopped and what kind of rails worked the best.

In 1862, President Abraham Lincoln signed a law creating the Union Pacific Railway Company, charging the company with laying a line all the way across the country. Before the transcontinental railway was completed, Americans traveled west in stagecoaches pulled by horses, or they sailed to Panama, where they could cross the narrow Central American isthmus quickly, and then sail the rest of the way to the west coast. It was therefore a very important occasion when workers, railroad officials, and politicians gathered to hammer in the golden spike signaling the completion of the transcontinental railway at Promontory Point in Utah on May 10, 1869.

The railroads grew quickly after that, and men and companies became rich and prosperous as the railroads fueled economic expansion throughout the United States. The labor unions, which had expanded

Union Pacific 119 at Promontory Point in Utah

as the railroads did, wanted to make sure the workers shared in the prosperity. They unified workers across the industry to demand better wages and working conditions.

Eugene V. Debs, who would later become a socialist leader and a friend of Carl Sandburg's, led a big strike in Chicago in 1894. All railroad service into and out of the city stopped when the workers walked off the job to demand better pay. President Grover Cleveland ordered U.S. Marshals and soldiers to break up the strike because it was interfering with the delivery of the U.S. mail. In the ensuing violence, thirteen workers were killed and millions of dollars in property was destroyed. Debs was sentenced to prison for interfering with the delivery of the mail.

In that same year, the song "I've Been Working on the Railroad" was first published. The song has been passed down through the generations ever since, and is still a favorite among children. Many a child has also been enthralled by the tale of John Henry, a mythical figure in American history who died as he raced a machine to dig a railroad tunnel through a mountain.

The tradition of great railroad stories and songs continued into the twentieth century, when Arlo Guthrie recorded probably the most popular train song ever, "The City of New Orleans." The lyrics evoke the power of the old railways and the pleasant rhythm of the train as it rumbles south from Illinois to the mouth of the Mississippi. "And the sons of Pullman porters and the sons of engineers / Ride their father's magic carpet made of steel,"[11] Guthrie sang in the 1972 hit. By then the history of the trains had to some extent come full circle. They were no longer so important, as more freight was moved in trucks and people tended to drive or fly when they traveled.

Still the trains—with all their mythology and power—will remain an integral part of the American landscape and history.

Before household refrigerators became available in the 1920s, ice blocks such as the ones being harvested here were used to keep food cool in the summer. Ice harvesting was difficult, dangerous work. As a young man, Sandburg moved ice blocks that weighed almost as much as he did.

Chapter
3

A Teenager in Hard Times

The early 1890s were hard times for the Sandburg family—and for the country. The economy became weak; many people were losing their jobs. The Sandburgs were used to frugality, but they cut down on the few luxuries to which they were accustomed. They used lard on their toast instead of butter. At Christmas, August Sandburg distributed the usual bag of candy and the oranges, but there were no toys for the children. "We honored the oranges by eating all the insides, pulp, and peelings," Carl wrote later.[1] Carl's older sister, Mary, stayed in school. The parents thought Mary might be able to get a good job as a teacher if she kept studying. Carl left school and began working full-time on a milk wagon. At the time, his little brother Freddie was two. Emil was seven. Carl and Emil played together, and Emil often asked Carl to read to him. Emil's favorite stories were Grimm's fairy tales, especially "The Knapsack, the Hat and the Horn."

Carl's mother woke him up every morning at 5:30. He ate pancakes, fried pork, and applesauce and then walked two miles to the dairy. Soon after he had started working on the milk wagon, Carl became sick with an extremely sore throat. He stayed home for two days and then went back to work. His brother, Martin, was also sick for a few days. Nobody worried too much about the sore throat that was going through the family until the two little brothers also became weak. Their throats hurt so badly they could not eat. The family brought their little bed into the house's kitchen, and laid the two boys together by the warm stove. The parents knew it would cost a lot of money, but they sent Carl to bring a doctor to the home. The doctor looked down the boys' throats and saw the characteristic gray film, or false membrane, of diphtheria. The doctor reported his diagnosis to the city officials, and the city health commissioner nailed a big red sign saying Diphtheria to the outside of the house. At the time people understood that diphtheria was contagious, and a vaccine had not yet been invented, so isolation was the only way to prevent the spread of the disease.

The two little boys grew weaker and weaker. The doctor came back and told the parents there was little they could do besides hope and pray. One afternoon, Freddie stopped breathing. As they mourned for Freddie, the family hoped that Emil, who was older and stronger, would pull through. Half an hour later Emil also stopped breathing. "Mother put her hands on him and said, 'Emil is gone, too,'" Carl wrote. "The grief hit us all hard."[2] The boys' bodies were placed in small white coffins and they were buried in the local cemetery. Carl and Martin cried themselves to sleep, then they woke in the middle of the night and cried some more. Carl said later that Freddie was so young when he died that he did not remember him very well, but he missed Emil for a long time. "For years I missed him and had my wonderings about what a chum and a younger brother he would have made," Carl wrote. "I can see now the lights in his blue eyes and over his wide freckled face and his quick beaming smile from a large mouth."[3]

After the two brothers died, the family's situation worsened. They owed money for funeral expenses and the burial plots in the cemetery. Carl kept working on the milk delivery wagon. That winter he worked in the freezing snow with just regular shoes. He did not have two dollars to spare for boots or one dollar to spare for rubber overshoes. His feet were cold all the time. The milk wagon job wore on him. Not only was he cold physically, but the owner was so quiet and grumpy that the job left Carl, who liked talkative, cheerful people, mentally depressed as well. Carl finally decided he had had enough and quit. The family had made it through the winter and Mary would soon graduate from high school and begin working as a teacher. Carl helped pay for a pretty white graduation dress, and then he began looking for a new job.

Carl thought getting a job as an apprentice would be ideal. Apprentices work for a person who has a skill, and they learn while they work. With the economy still weak, there were few openings for apprentices. Finally Carl found work in a drugstore, running errands and stocking shelves. It was at the pharmacy job that he had his first taste of alcohol, finding whiskey quite awful but rum "so grand and insinuating and soft and ticklish."[4] He liked the pharmacy job but saw that it would not lead to a profession, so he decided maybe he could work his way into a job as a barber.

He started as an assistant at a barbershop, cleaning floors, shining shoes, and occasionally helping customers by brushing their clothes and helping them with baths in an adjoining bathing room. Carl would often get a 25-cent tip after getting a bath ready and scrubbing a customer's back with a brush. At that job, the artful young man realized he could sneak into a nearby bar at lunchtime and eat lunch for free. Although he was clever about sneaking food, Carl got grief for months when he made a big mistake. He had a stiff brush he used to brush people's coats and hats. Once a man came in wearing a silk hat. Carl took it off the rack and began brushing it with the stiff brush. The man grabbed the hat out of his hand and looked at Carl as if he were a dangerous criminal. Carl had no idea that only soft brushes should be used on silk hats, but after that incident he obtained a brush that was so soft it could hardly be felt as he brushed it across his fingers.

Finally Carl's job search came full circle when he went back to work on a milk wagon. This time it was for Sam Barlow, who was more talkative than Carl's earlier milk wagon boss. They talked about their customers, politics, and religion. Barlow amused Carl with his little jokes about people. One young man Barlow knew couldn't quite seem to get his life going. "He never gets started," Barlow said. "He's always getting ready to begin to start to commence."[5] They worked well together and Carl especially enjoyed the hearty lunches Barlow's wife provided every day. He stayed with Barlow for more than a year, learning how to solicit new customers, take good care of the horses, and make sure the milk was always clean and sanitary. At the end of the year, Carl decided to look for a new job; he wanted to find one that would lead to a profession, but those seemed to be few and far between.

Carl thought he was lucky when a tinner, or man who works making things out of metal, offered him a job as an apprentice. The tinner turned out to be a drunkard, and after Carl had gone to the shop a few times and found it closed, he gave up on that job.

The hardest job Carl had lasted only two weeks, but he remembered it for the rest of his life. When the temperature dropped down to around zero on Lake George, the Glenwood Ice Company called for night help with the ice harvest. Before electric refrigeration was invented, ice was used to cool food and prevent it from spoiling. For the first week, Carl was a floater. He stood on top of big rafts of ice and propelled them toward a machine that would cut them into blocks. He had never worked outdoors at night before, and he was fascinated to see how the stars moved across the sky. The Big Dipper would start out on one side of the sky and slowly, as the night wore on, move all the way across the sky. "I did my wondering about how that spread of changing stars was made, how long it took to make, how long it could last, and how little any of us is standing and looking up at it," he wrote later.[6]

The second week of the ice harvest was much more difficult. Carl was assigned to the icehouse, where he had to use big tongs to move heavy blocks of ice into neat piles. The blocks weighed almost as much as Carl did, and trying to move them all night was physically the hardest work he had ever done. When he arrived home in the morning, after working all night, his body was too exhausted to sleep. As the week wore on, he was able to sleep better, but then he had strange dreams. One day, he dreamed the house was on fire. He jumped out of bed and ran out of the house, yelling about the fire. His mother just smiled, saying that she had had dreams that had fooled her, too. Carl said that if he dreamed the house was on fire again, he would just roll over and let it burn.

Carl was not in school as a teenager, but that did not mean his learning stopped. He read his sister Mary's schoolbooks, especially John Fiske's *Civil Government in the United States*. He read the newspapers. He and Martin sat in the kitchen and read sayings and jokes from *Hostetter's Illustrated United States Almanac*. The almanac had jokes such as: "'Are you in favor of enlarging the curriculum?' asked a rural school director of a farmer in his district. 'Enlarge nothing,' replied the old gentleman. 'The building's big enough; what we want to do is teach more things to the children.'"[7]

There were also travel-ing speakers who held mass meetings. Sandburg's favorite was William Jen-nings Bryan, a populist and orator who was best known for his opposition to the gold standard. He believed that if the government used more silver to mint more money, the working classes would benefit. Inflation would make it easier for farmers and others to pay their debts to banks. Bryan expounded his theory in his "Cross of Gold" speech at the Democratic National Convention of 1896. He won the Democratic nomination

William Jennings Bryan was born in 1860 and died in 1925. Sandburg admired Bryan's speaking talent and populism.

again two more times, but was defeated at the national election. "I followed his speeches across the country and I heard him speak in Galesburg and in Monmouth," Carl remembered. "He was my hero, the Man of the People who spoke for the right, and against him were the Enemies of the People. He opened his mouth and the words pouring out were, for me in that year, truth and gospel. Later I would find out that he was a voice, an orator, an actor, a singer and not much of a thinker."[8]

Carl also found time to play. He had a gang of friends who called themselves the Dirty Dozen. They did not usually get into trouble, but one hot summer day the group decided to go swimming at a pond they thought was a public swimming hole. They had just removed their clothes when the Galesburg police chief drove up and arrested the group. Carl and Martin were horrified, thinking that their parents would never forgive them for getting in trouble with the law, but the judge decided the police chief had been a little overzealous and sent the boys home with a lecture about not swimming without authorization. Carl's parents seemed to feel the same way and did not punish the boys.

Carl did not travel a lot in his youth. Once he and his friends scraped together five dollars and bought one horse for three dollars and another horse for two dollars. They borrowed a wagon and drove the horses about fifty miles to the Illinois River, where they swam, fished, and camped. The three-dollar horse died, and the teenagers buried him "with respect and many jokes."[9] They were surprised that it had been the three-dollar horse that died, rather than the two-dollar horse. They scraped their pockets and spent five dollars on another horse and drove the pair home; adventure completed. When Carl was sixteen, his father gave him a pass to take the train to Peoria. He went alone, and felt very grown up as he explored the unfamiliar streets.

Later he went to Chicago—again with a pass from his father. He walked for hours and soaked up the hustle and bustle of the big city. He visited the offices of the newspapers he had delivered for years, took in a vaudeville show, and saw the Board of Trade, where traders pointed fingers and yelled prices as they speculated in commodities such as grain futures and pork bellies. When he returned, he tried to explain what he had liked about Chicago but his family could not understand.

Carl loved baseball and played it whenever he could. He followed the sport avidly, easily committing to memory the top professional players' batting averages and the records of the best pitchers. "There were times when my head seemed empty of everything but baseball names and figures," Carl remembered later.[10] For a time, he played more seriously because he harbored a secret ambition to become a professional baseball player. One day he and a friend were practicing in a pasture. His friend hit a high fly ball. Carl ran as fast as he could to catch it. He imagined himself making the kind of athletic, diving catches that got a player noticed by the baseball scouts. Suddenly, he fell, his foot screaming in pain. He looked down and realized he had stepped in a hole with a broken beer bottle inside. He sat there in agony for a few minutes. Then he walked to the doctor's office. The doctor cleaned the deep gash on his foot very carefully and then put in four stitches.

After that, Carl still loved baseball, but he no longer dreamed of becoming a professional player. He did not know what he wanted to do, or what he wanted to be. He did not like the choices that Galesburg offered. He did not have the education that would help him find a better job elsewhere. It was a tough time for Carl, and he did not know what to do. Finally, he decided to do something strange.

Diphtheria

Diphtheria is now a rare disease in the United States, but before modern medicine, it was a notorious killer, especially among children. In the early 1700s, a diphtheria epidemic swept through New England, killing hundreds of children. The disease was also prevalent in the British royal family in the 1800s, killing Queen Victoria's daughter and granddaughter in 1878. In the 1800s diptheria fatality rates were as high as 90 percent.

Diphtheria starts out with a fever and a sore throat. A bacterium spreads through the mouth tissues and begins to grow a false membrane, or type of skin, across the throat. Victims die of asphyxiation, or not being able to breathe. It is highly contagious, easily transmitted through inhaling bacterial particles or touching surfaces that have been contaminated with the bacteria.

French doctor Pierre Bretonneau named the disease in 1826, taking the name from the Greek word for leather, which seemed to describe the characteristic membrane that grows over the throat. He treated diphtheria with a tracheotomy, or cutting a hole in the patient's windpipe at the front of the neck. Doctors at the time were just beginning to understand that diseases were spread by tiny organisms such as bacteria and viruses. Joseph O'Dwyer, an American doctor, was known for coming up with a new treatment for diphtheria when he discovered in 1888 that a tube inserted into diphtheria patients' throats could allow them to continue breathing. Emil Von Behring, a German doctor, discovered an antitoxin, or medicine, in the 1890s. Von Behring won the Nobel Prize for medicine in 1901 for his discovery.

In 1925, in the isolated Alaskan town of Nome, Dr. Curtis Welch rushed to the bedside of two very ill Eskimo children and found they were so ill that he could not examine their mouths. They died the next day. Welch saw another child with the telltale gray blotches on his throat. He realized he needed to treat the entire town with the diphtheria antitoxin, which would help those who were already sick and prevent the disease from spreading. The antitoxin was about 900 miles away in Anchorage. It was shipped by train about 220 miles to Nenana. Teams of sled dogs brought the medicine from Nenana 674 miles to Nome. Welch treated everyone in the village with the medicine, preventing a terrible epidemic.

The famous Iditarod sled dog race, which is held every winter, commemorates the intrepid mushers, or dogsled operators, who brought the medicine through the Alaskan winter to Nome. Balto, the dog who led the last sled as it arrived in Nome, became a celebrity. Universal Studios released an animated feature film about the dog in 1995.

Sandburg's two younger brothers died of diphtheria before this antitoxin became widely available. Diphtheria and many other contagious diseases are now controlled with vaccines.

The development of treatments and vaccines for diphtheria began speeding up in the twentieth century. In 1913, Dr. Béla Schick in Hungary discovered a test that shows whether a person is immune to diphtheria. A person who survives diphtheria usually has lifetime immunity to the disease.

By the 1920s, vaccines against smallpox and rabies had already been discovered. Two British scientists, Alexander Glenny and Barbara Hopkins, were studying diphtheria. One of their containers was too large too fit in the autoclave, a machine for sterilizing medical equipment. They cleaned the container with formalin, a liquid containing formaldehyde. They discovered that the diphtheria toxin that had been in contact with the formalin was weak; it could be injected into the scientists' guinea pigs without harming them. Another scientist, Gaston Ramon, working at the Pasteur Institute in France, continued the research and further developed the vaccination using a heating technique that minimized the toxicity, or dangerousness, of the vaccination.

Though science was progressing, diphtheria remained a sometimes fatal disease. In the United States in 1920, doctors reported 148,000 cases of diphtheria and 13,000 deaths.

Doctors began administering the vaccination widely in the 1950s, along with vaccinations against tetanus and pertusis, or whooping cough. All three diseases, which once terrorized communities, have become rare. Only five cases of diphtheria were reported in the United States between 1980 and 2006. It is also rare in the rest of the world, though there was a severe outbreak in the former Soviet Union in 1993 and 1994, in which about 5,000 people died. Political turmoil had led to the breakdown in systems for delivering vaccinations.

Theodore Roosevelt, who would later become the twenty-sixth U.S. president, led his Rough Riders unit into battle in Cuba. Sandburg marched with the U.S. Army across Puerto Rico as the Spanish-American War was winding down.

Chapter 4

A Hobo and a Soldier

Carl Sandburg's parents did not like the idea, but in June of 1887, Carl threw $3.25, a watch, a knife, a pipe, a bar of soap, a comb, a razor, a small mirror, and a few handkerchiefs in his pockets and set off to explore the country. Clara Sandburg cried, and August Sandburg looked scornful as Carl walked out the door of his home in Galesburg and headed toward the rail yard. As a freight train rumbled slowly by on its way west, he grabbed on to an open boxcar and jumped in. The train took him past miles and miles of new cornfields to the Mississippi River, where Sandburg feasted his eyes on the sight of America's longest river. The train crossed the Mississippi and slowed down in Fort Madison, Iowa, about sixty-five miles later, and Sandburg jumped off. He had ridden the rails illegally for the first time and had survived. He was not alone. Ever since the Panic of 1893, legions of men had crisscrossed the United States, sneaking rides in freight cars and forming rural outposts where they shared food, stories, and information. The campgrounds were called "hobo jungles." Most of the men were honest; they were looking for work and wanted to explore the country. But among the hobos—as Sandburg would soon learn—were thieves and robbers.

A steamboat foreman in Fort Madison offered Sandburg passage to Keokuk, another town about twenty miles downriver, in exchange for unloading barrels of nails when they arrived. Sandburg sailed down the Mississippi to Keokuk, where he met his first fellow hobo. The man explained to him that people will give hobos "lumps," or bread and meat wrapped in newspaper. The hobo had three lumps, so he gave one to Sandburg. They sat and Sandburg's new friend told him about notorious hobos he had known, and how some towns were especially hostile—only he said "horstyle"—to hobos. Sandburg walked away when the man appeared to be getting too friendly and spent the night in the basement of a house that was under construction in Keokuk. In the morning he found an old tomato can and had it filled with asphalt for fifteen cents. He bought an inexpensive brush and went from home to home, offering to blacken stoves for a meal or a small fee. After a few days, there did not seem to be anybody who needed their stoves blackened, and Sandburg saw a sign in a restaurant window that said "Waiter Wanted."

Sandburg entered the little restaurant and the owner hired him immediately, for fifty cents a day. The owner showed him the restaurant's simple menu and then he left, saying he would be back in a little while. Sandburg prepared meals of eggs and ham sandwiches for the customers. When the owner returned, he appeared to be slightly drunk. He said he would come back again, and when he did, he was obviously drunk, and fell asleep at one of the tables. Sandburg quietly closed up the restaurant, took fifty cents out of the cash register, and left.

He continued riding the rails west to Bean Lake, Missouri. There he worked on a railroad section gang, swinging a pick to build railroads for ten hours a day, and then swinging a scythe to cut weeds for ten hours a day. The crew ate a breakfast of side pork, potatoes, and coffee; a lunch of side pork, potatoes, and coffee; and a dinner of side pork, potatoes, and coffee. After two weeks, Sandburg had had enough of the monotonous diet and the exhausting work, and he pressed on to Kansas City.

In Kansas City he found work as a dishwasher at a friendly restaurant where a charming cook would make him anything he wanted to eat and George, the waiter, sang beautifully. "George could sing either old time songs or late hits. One afternoon he sang a sad song that had me melting,"

Sandburg wrote later.[1] After two weeks, Sandburg took off again, but this time it was harder; he had enjoyed the good food and the good music.

At about this time, Sandburg's brother Martin, back in Galesburg, read in the newspaper about an unidentified hobo being killed when a train ran over him. Martin feared that it was his brother, who was writing only infrequent letters home. Sandburg did run into trouble, but it was not fatal. He was riding another freight train when a brakeman told him to either pay or accept the consequences. Sandburg refused to pay and the brakeman punched him so hard that blood flowed from his nose. Other brakemen were kinder and would simply tell him to stay out of sight.

Hobos were a common sight during the Great Depression. Some hobos traveled from job to job, while others avoided work. Sandburg joined the ranks of the working hobos for about four months in 1887.

Sandburg made a point of visiting the Swedish town of Lindsborg, in Kansas. As a child of Swedish immigrants and a member of the Swedish Lutheran Church, he thought it was important to visit a town that was predominantly Swedish. He found a farm that needed help with their harvest and asked if he could sleep in the hayloft. The next morning, just as he was opening his eyes, he heard a Swedish voice say, "Is that bum up yet?" "The first time in my life I had heard myself referred to as a bum was among Swedes I had made a detour

35

to see. . . . To him I was a bum and he was giving me no such hand of fellowship as George or the chef in the Kansas City kitchen," Sandburg recalled later.[2]

He had a close call when he encountered a man who was holding up hobos with his pistol and robbing them of all their money. The robber seemed to like Sandburg and did not threaten to shoot or rob him.

After a few days on the Swedish farm, Sandburg continued his way west. In Lakin, Kansas, he worked for three weeks harvesting wheat. Then it was west again to Colorado, where he was amazed to see the Rocky Mountains rising in front of him. Riding back to Denver one night after visiting Canyon City, Sandburg had another brush with danger. There were no empty freight cars on the train, so he was standing on the coupling between two trains. He thought he was fine, but suddenly he realized he had slept a few seconds. For the next few frightening hours, he made himself move constantly in order to stay awake. For years afterward, he remembered the night he almost fell under a train to his death: "Many a time later I said that the Angel of Death hovered over that train that night and saw me standing and sleeping and brushed past me with soft wing tips saying, 'Not yet for this boy. He's young yet. Let him live.'"[3]

Sandburg continued traveling back east, working temporary jobs and hanging out in hobo jungles. His life as a hobo had exposed him to the good, the bad, and the ugly of the American Midwest. He had learned a measure of self-confidence and realized that he did not always have to be as shy with people as was his custom. "I was getting a deeper self-respect than I had in Galesburg, so much I knew," he wrote. "I was getting to be a better story teller. You can be loose and easy when from day to day you meet strangers you will know only an hour or a day or two."[4]

On October 15, 1897, about four months after he had left, Sandburg returned home. He had fifteen dollars in his pocket and lots of stories and experiences in his mind. He knew he was ready for new challenges, but he was not sure what to do. He thought about enlisting in the armed services, but at the time there was a three-year minimum commitment, and that seemed too long.

Circumstances would change quickly. Sandburg was working as an apprentice painter when tensions between the United States and Spain over the political status of Cuba, an island nation ninety miles off the Florida coast in the Caribbean, erupted in the wake of an explosion. The *Maine*, a battleship that had been sent to the port of Havana to protect American citizens and interests, blew up, and all 260 crew members were killed. The United States declared war on Spain on April 20, 1898, and Sandburg, like thousands of young men all over the United States, enlisted. He signed up for Company C, Sixth Infantry Regiment, Illinois volunteers. He claimed to be twenty-one but he was really twenty years old.

Sandburg and his fellow Galesburg volunteers first gathered at the fairgrounds in Springfield, the capital of Illinois and the hometown of one of Sandburg's heroes, Abraham Lincoln. They slept in a fairgrounds building that normally housed prize rabbits and cows, and started getting ready for battle. They were each given a blue wool Civil War-era uniform. These uniforms had been designed to keep soldiers warm during American winters, and were not ideal for the soldiers' tropical destinations. Sandburg recalled, "This was the same uniform that the privates under Grant and Sherman had worn thirty-five years before, intended for wear in those border states of the South where snow fell and zero weather might come. . . . I felt honored to wear the uniform of the famous Union armies and yet I had a mistrust of it."[5] When he had free time in Springfield, he explored the streets of the city on foot, a habit that would become a life-long custom. He stopped by the historic Lincoln home.

The men continued on to Camp Russell A. Alger near Washington, D.C., where they slept in tents and continued their training. Sandburg noted years later that the conditions at the camp were pretty awful.

The open latrines the men used smelled horrible, and he sometimes saw the cook scraping maggots off the meat he was preparing for the men. Amid these conditions, he noticed—without much apparent bitterness—that one captain was feeding his dog sirloin steaks.

During their free time, Sandburg and his tent mate, Andrew Tanning, visited the Ford Theatre, where John Wilkes Booth had assassinated

Abraham Lincoln, and the Petersen's Boarding House, where Lincoln was taken after the shooting. Sandburg recited lines from Lincoln's favorite poem, "Oh, Why Should the Spirit of a Mortal Be Proud." The poem, by William Knox, begins:

> Oh, why should the spirit of a mortal be proud?
> Like a swift-flitting meteor, a fast-flying cloud,
> A flash of the lightning, a break of the wave,
> He passeth from life to his rest in the grave.[6]

From Camp Alger the company traveled by train to Charleston, South Carolina, where they boarded the *Rita* and sailed for Cuba. They stopped at Guantánamo, but there they heard that the Cuban city of Santiago had already been won by the Americans and that they would not fight there. They sailed on to Guánica, Puerto Rico. While the conditions at Camp Alger had not been very comfortable, Sandburg and his fellow soldiers found true hardship in Puerto Rico. Though they did not have to fight the Spanish, they found that Puerto Rican mosquitoes attacked ferociously. Many of the soldiers had both eyes swollen almost shut from mosquito bites. Sandburg remembered that he would sleep with a rubber poncho over his head to shield him from the bites, then wake up with a headache from breathing stale air. "They were mosquitoes of the type you say, 'One could kill a dog, two could kill a man,' " Sandburg recalled.[7] Rations were canned beans and hardtack, a hard biscuit that was used extensively in the Civil War because it would last without spoiling.

The men marched from Guánica about twenty-five miles along the southern coast of Puerto Rico to Ponce. From there they headed north into the Cordillera Central, the central mountains of Puerto Rico. They marched uphill, each man carrying fifty pounds of equipment, including wool blankets, wearing heavy wool uniforms in the humid tropical heat of August. Men became desperately tired; they sometimes threw half or all of their blankets to the side of the road to lessen their loads. Sandburg kept his spirits up. He sang an old army song that went, "Oh, I'm glad I'm in the army, I'm glad I'm in today. . . ." He picked up a few words of Spanish from local people they passed. He noticed they seemed pleased to be out from under 400 years of rule by Spain.

After marching thirty-two miles in a few days from Ponce to Utuado in central Puerto Rico, the soldiers were told that an agreement leading up to a peace treaty had been signed, and that they would not have to fight. They marched back down the mountain to Ponce and sailed for New York, ragged, hungry, and thin, but alive. When Sandburg walked off the boat in New York, he bought milk and a loaf of bread and enjoyed them almost ecstatically. "As I ate that bread and milk I felt that I had been an animal and was now a human being—it was so clean, tasty, delicious."[8]

Company C returned by train to Galesburg, where they were welcomed with special dances, dinners, and speeches. Sandburg went to visit his sister Mary at the country school where she was teaching. She gave him a nice bed to sleep on, and he dropped into it gratefully. After tossing and turning for half the night, he rolled onto the floor, where he slept peacefully until morning. Sandburg went home to show his delighted parents his discharge papers commending his service and his pay of $103.73. August Sandburg was so pleased with his son's discharge certificate—which said, "a good soldier, service honest and faithful"—that he framed it and hung it on the wall.

Sandburg had wandered west and seen a wide swath of his country. He had traveled east and seen more, including a tropical island. Now it was time to find out what he could make of himself.

The Spanish-American War

The Spanish-American war was not a very large conflict militarily, but it represented an important point in the history of both countries. The United States emerged from the war—somewhat controversially—as a modern military power with dominion as far away as the Philippines. Spain came through having lost the last remnants of its once vast intercontinental empire.

Spain had been a great colonial power, ruling territories from the southern tip of what is now Chile all the way north to the United States. A series of wars and rebellions in the early 1800s had led to independence for most of Spain's former colonies. In 1898, Spain still ruled the Philippines, Puerto Rico, and Cuba. Cuban nationalists had fought Spanish forces from 1868 to 1878. That war ended with a peace treaty in which Spain promised to respect Cuba's desire for self-rule.

From 1881 to 1895 José Martí, a poet and longtime believer in Cuban independence, lived in New York, where he published a newspaper, spoke out in support of the Cuban revolution against Spain, and organized support for a military attack. In 1895, he led a small army against the more than 100,000 troops attempting to maintain Spanish control of the island. Spanish general Valeriano Weyler y Nicolau, who would later become known as "the Butcher," easily defeated Martí's forces, then locked thousands of Cubans up in concentration camps, where they suffered from illness, exposure, and starvation.

American newspapers, which were growing as businesses and fighting one another for gains in circulation, or readership, reported aggressively on the conflict in Cuba. General Weyler was brutal, but sometimes the newspapers, in their drive for readership and pro-war passion, exaggerated even the horrors of Spanish repression in Cuba. Tensions continued to escalate, leading President William McKinley to send the *Maine* to the port of Havana, the capital of Cuba. The ship exploded on February 15, 1898, and most of the crew was killed. Many years later, a Navy investigation suggested that the coal on the ship might have spontaneously combusted, or burst into flame, but at the time, the explosion greatly heightened war fever in the United States. William Randolph Hearst, owner of the *New York Journal*, was famous for the way the *Journal* and his other newspapers aggressively covered Spanish atrocities and promoted the war. After the *Maine* exploded, Hearst published a million copies of a special issue dedicated to the conflict in Cuba. "Remember the *Maine!*" became the national battle cry.

McKinley declared war on Spain, but the small American Navy was no match for the enormous Spanish forces marshaled on the island. The United States decided to blockade Cuba, to prevent supply ships from arriving, while it built up its fighting forces. For that reason, the

U.S. Navy ended up also going to the Philippines, a Spanish-controlled nation near Australia in the Pacific Ocean. The blockade strategy worked, however, and Spanish forces were fairly easily defeated in Cuba. A force of about 16,500 American soldiers landed in Cuba on June 20. On July 1, they fought the Spanish forces at El Caney and San Juan Hill.

A surgeon attends to the wounded in a field hospital during the Spanish-American War.

Theodore Roosevelt, who would later be elected president, recalled that leading his "Rough Riders" into battle on San Juan Hill was the best day of his life.

The attacks did not seem very successful to the Americans, and indeed, 280 Americans were killed and 1,500 wounded. Even so, the Spanish forces panicked and surrendered. American forces later marched through Puerto Rico, encountering only token resistance. In the Philippines, where locals had been fighting Spain, the Americans also routed Spain easily, but found themselves locked in a long battle with the Filipinos, who wanted self-rule and independence.

The United States fought the Philippine insurrection for two years in one of the most controversial aspects of the United States' involvement in the Spanish-American War. Mark Twain, who wrote *The Adventures of Tom Sawyer*, was one of the many writers and speakers who opposed the United States' war against the Philippine nationalists. Repeatedly, Twain spoke against the war in the Philippines, claiming, "We have debauched America's honor and blackened her face before the world."[9]

The Spanish-American war ended on December 10, 1898, when, under the terms of a peace treaty signed in France, Spain formally yielded control of the Philippines, Puerto Rico, Guam, and Cuba to the United States. The United States paid Spain $20 million. It had taken just 120 years for the United States to change from being a small colony fighting its own revolution for independence from Britain to becoming an imperial power that would ruthlessly put down the Philippine revolution in the coming two years. Many observers celebrated the change, while others were critical of it.

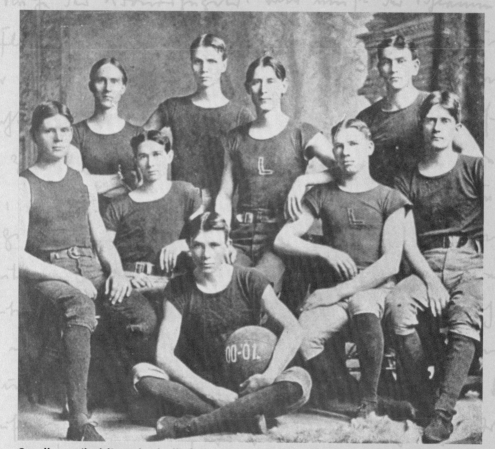

Sandburg (holding the ball) followed baseball avidly as a boy, but in college, he excelled at the recently invented sport of basketball. He played right guard on the Lombard team for four seasons, and wrote later that he enjoyed every minute. He was also elected editor in chief of the college newspaper.

Chapter
5

A Restless Young Man

When Sandburg returned from the war, a friend told him that veterans could attend Lombard College for free. Sandburg jumped at the chance. He was admitted as a student to the college's preparatory school, or high school, with permission to take college classes as well.

One of his first classes was English literature. He had to read poetry by Robert Browning, an English poet whom Sandburg came to adore. He enjoyed Browning's poetry so much, he memorized his favorite verses. He was fascinated by the power of writers like Charles Lamb, an English writer and critic whose descriptions of London a hundred years earlier were so apt that Sandburg felt as though he had actually traveled in time and space to England a century earlier.

American literature was considered new and young at the time, and Sandburg was assigned just a few American authors. He noticed the name Walt Whitman in a book of critical essays and looked for Whitman's classic book of poetry, *Leaves of Grass*. He found a second-hand copy of the book and discovered a kind of poetry that spoke to him more intimately than any other poetry he had read. Whitman, who died in 1892, became a longtime influence on Sandburg, who could not get enough of Whitman's bold, unconventional style and his love of the American landscape.

For years Sandburg had seen Philip Green Wright walk back and forth to the college from his home in Galesburg. As a student, Sandburg finally met the versatile, charming professor who not only taught mathematics, astronomy, and economics but also directed the college's athletic programs. Wright was also a political radical who encouraged Sandburg to think about politics. The professor organized the Poor Writer's Club, for which students would gather at his house to eat snacks and read one another's work. The two men got along well from the start, and Sandburg would always remember Wright as a mentor who had faith in him.

After his first year at Lombard, he was surprised to find that the ninety members of Company C had asked their U.S. representative, George W. Prince, to appoint Sandburg as the district's representative to West Point, the U.S. Army's prestigious military academy in New York. Sandburg had never dreamed of becoming a high-ranking member of the military, but he could not resist the support of all the members of his old company. "There was something about the way the Company C officers picked me out of ninety and more others—I had to go along with them," he wrote.[1]

Sandburg had to take a test and compete with other students to make his appointment permanent, and he was at a disadvantage with his lack of formal schooling. He struggled with the exam and failed arithmetic and, ironically, grammar. Among the students admitted to the class, and an example of the type of student with whom Sandburg was competing, was Douglas MacArthur. MacArthur, who had studied with tutors, aced the entrance exams and went on to become a famous World War II general.

Soon Sandburg was back in school at Lombard, involved in everything from classes to theater to sports. Basketball had been invented only a few years earlier, in 1891, when a Springfield, Massachusetts, physical education teacher nailed some peach baskets to a gymnasium wall and invented rules for a game he thought would help keep the school's athletes in shape during the winter. Basketball quickly became popular throughout the country, and Lombard College fielded a team that played against other local colleges. Sandburg, who was always naturally athletic and competitive, learned the game quickly and played for Lombard's team for four years. Lombard won its second game after he joined the team, 16 to 12, against its cross-town rival, Knox College. Sportswriters at the time noted Sandburg's leadership ability and his aggressive defensive play.

Oratory, or public speaking, was an important kind of entertainment in the days before movies and television became widespread. Sandburg admired the great speakers of the day and wanted to become like them. He took classes in elocution, or public speaking, and prepared for the college's annual speaking contest. The first year he competed, he wrote a speech on polar explorers and the Vikings. He memorized the speech and practiced. When his turn came, he did well until about halfway through, when he forgot what he was supposed to say.

The next year, Sandburg wrote a speech titled "A Man with Ideals" on John Ruskin, an English writer and reformer. Sandburg liked Ruskin's ideas about the harm the Industrial Revolution had done to humankind's artistic sensibilities. He warned, "Factories crush the human body and darken the human soul. Men by thousands are killing each other, driven by greed and covetousness."[2] This time Sandburg memorized the speech and delivered it perfectly, winning the Swan prize for the best performance of an original speech. It was an important moment in Sandburg's life. He realized that when he believed something strongly, his performance could be excellent.

Sandburg had one frightening time during his otherwise superb college career. In the spring of 1901, he began to have difficulty with his vision. He went to an eye doctor, who diagnosed him with pterygium, a condition in which the skin around the eye starts growing across the cornea, eventually affecting vision. Its cause is not known, but the condition is more common in people who are outside a lot and exposed to sun, wind, and dust. Eye surgery was not advanced in 1901, and the operation to remove the tissue growing into his eye was dangerous. However, the surgery went well, and after staying in bed for two weeks to let the incision heal, Sandburg was thrilled to find that he could see well again.

Sandburg developed a strong friendship with Fred Dickinson, a fellow student who shared his interest in writing and reading. The two men worked together on a book celebrating the fiftieth anniversary of Lombard College. They wrote articles, found pictures, designed pages, and did hundreds of other chores involved in producing a volume about the school's history. They enjoyed the work together and learned about publishing. Dickinson also introduced Sandburg to work as a stereoscope salesperson. During one summer, the two went to the Detroit area to sell the machines, which showed stereographs, or two photographs taken from slightly different angles that would appear as a three-dimensional image when viewed through the stereoscope. Viewmasters, a small plastic toy still in use today, are a kind of modern-day stereoscope. Before radios and televisions became widespread, the stereoscopes were a popular form of home entertainment. Sandburg liked the machines, and he enjoyed going door to door trying to interest local families in purchasing the technology and the pictures.

During his fourth year, he seemed to be everywhere at Lombard College. He sang in the glee club, played on the basketball team, and edited the school newspaper and its literary magazine, the *Lombard Review*. He was popular with his professors and fellow students. When the school year came to an end in 1902, Sandburg decided it was enough. To earn a degree, he would have had to stay for a year or two more, but he felt he had gained much in four years and that it was time to move on. It was not unusual in those days to leave college without a degree.

Because he had not earned a degree in any particular field, the next few years would be difficult as Sandburg explored different kinds of work, literature, and writing, and tried to figure out what to do next. At the time, he wrote, "I was only sure that in the years ahead I would read many books and I would be a writer and try my hand at many kinds of writing."[3]

Sandburg became a wanderer. He sold stereoscope views in New Jersey, returned to work as a firefighter in Galesburg, and lived in Chicago. In Chicago he attended events at the Whitman Cultural Center and worked on the center's magazine. All the time he was reading and writing and exploring different careers. He recopied poems that were particularly important to him into his voluminous notebooks. One such notebook contained Walt Whitman's "Song of the Open Road," with its stirring lines, including, "All seems beautiful to me."

Once, traveling by freight train from New Jersey to Chicago, Sandburg was arrested and thrown into jail in Pittsburgh, Pennsylvania. The charge was riding a freight car without buying a ticket and the sentence was ten days. In a letter to his old professor, Philip Green Wright, Sandburg noted that the warden received fifty cents a day to feed each prisoner, but seemed to spend five cents at the most. "For breakfast, we had a half loaf of bread, and a cup of hot brown water masquerading as coffee; for luncheon a half loaf of stale bread again, soup on Wednesday and Saturday; for dinner—there was no dinner."[4]

Sandburg was not the only young writer of his time who saw the inside of a jail. Jack London was born to a poor single mother in California in 1876 and, like Sandburg, went to work following elementary school. Traveling the United States as a hobo and going to the Yukon Territory during the Gold Rush, London had spectacular success as a novelist and short story writer. Sandburg read and reread London's best works, such as *The Call of the Wild* and *The Sea-Wolf*. Although Sandburg was living the chaotic life of a wanderer, he kept working at his writing and his speaking. *Thistle*, a small poetry magazine, published one of his first poems, "The Falling Leaves." Sandburg wrote the poem in a conventional, rhyming style:

> Thus earth-bound soul protests and grieves
> > Yet down beneath its pride,
> Yet deeper than the hint of leaves
> > speak slow, "Have faith! Abide."[5]

Professor Wright bought a small, hand-operated press and installed it in his basement. Sandburg collected various poems and short essays and sent them to Wright, who published them as Sandburg's first book, a small volume titled *In Reckless Ecstasy*. Sandburg wrote a speech on Walt Whitman, and a few other talks on topics such as the development of the English language and the travesties of human history. He tried to have himself hired as a speaker and was praised for some of his public appearances, but he could not at the time develop a full schedule of speeches. Meanwhile, his brother Martin had married and settled down in Galesburg. Mary continued to work as a teacher. Carl sometimes felt bad about his wandering ways. He had a recurring nightmare in which a horse he was riding at full speed suddenly vanished. Still, he continued this lifestyle for five years, going from one place to another, from one kind of work to another.

Walt Whitman

One of the giants of American letters had a decidedly strange career in which he repeatedly edited and rewrote his first work. Walt Whitman was born on Long Island, New York, in 1819. His main work of poetry, *Leaves of Grass*, was a pioneering collection of free verse that celebrated America in unprecedented ways. For many years, he rewrote and republished *Leaves of Grass*, always trying to improve the poems.

Whitman attended elementary school for six years. As a young teenager, he went to work as an apprentice printer. He worked at newspapers in New York City for several years, and then became a schoolteacher. Although he had little formal education, he read voraciously on his own. He also loved to attend the theater and the opera in New York City.

In those years before the Civil War, Americans were becoming very divided over slavery, which was legal throughout the American South. Whitman went to New Orleans and witnessed slave auctions and slavery firsthand. He became a fervent opponent of slavery. He returned to New York City a staunch member of the Free Soil party, which was pushing for slavery to be illegal in any new state to join the United States. He became editor of the *Brooklyn Eagle*, but was later fired because the newspaper owners disagreed with his antislavery stance.

Whitman began working on *Leaves of Grass* and published the first edition in 1855. He continued revising the poems in *Leaves of Grass* as the conflict over slavery grew deeper. When the Civil War broke out in 1861, Whitman's younger brother, George, joined the Union forces. A year later, a newspaper article said he was among the wounded at the battle of Fredericksburg. Whitman, who was forty-three at the time, went to Washington to look for his wounded brother. After searching the military hospitals for two weeks with no luck, Whitman received permission to go to an army camp in Virginia. There he was delighted to find his brother with only a slight scratch on his jaw. On his way back to Washington, D.C., army officials asked him to help transfer the wounded to hospitals in the city. He did so and ended up staying there for the rest of the Civil War, working for the government and helping care for the injured soldiers. He also wrote articles and poetry about the often chaotic rhythms of life in wartime Washington.

When President Abraham Lincoln was assassinated on April 14, 1865, shortly after the end of the Civil War, Whitman wrote one of his most famous poems, "O Captain! My Captain!" The poem conveys Whitman's admiration of Lincoln's leadership—especially his successful leadership during the war—and Whitman's sadness at his death.

"From fearful trip, the victor ship, comes in with object won; / Exult, O shores, and ring, O bells! / But I, with mournful tread, / Walk the deck my Captain lies, / Fallen cold and dead."[6]

Walt Whitman

After the war, Whitman continued to write and rewrite *Leaves of Grass*. He worked as a clerk in Washington until a stroke in 1873 left him partially paralyzed. He moved to Camden, New Jersey, where he lived until his death in 1892. As an older man, Whitman composed important works of prose, including *Democratic Vistas*, about democracy, and another book about his Civil War experiences, *Specimen Days & Collect*.

Although Whitman has long been considered a giant of American literature, he has always been somewhat controversial. In his own time, the great writer Henry David Thoreau complained that Whitman's poems sometimes seemed to focus on sex at the expense of love. Although Whitman never openly declared that he was homosexual, his poems often seemed to celebrate sexual encounters between men. Gay liberation activists made Whitman their hero in the 1970s, in some ways reigniting the controversy over Whitman's poetry.

After the terrorist attacks on the United States on September 11, 2001, National Public Radio attempted to comfort the nation by broadcasting a recitation of Whitman's "Song of Myself." Four years later, readers, writers, and poets in the United States celebrated the 150th anniversary of *Leaves of Grass*, showing that Whitman's pioneering free verse and love for his country were enduring.

Carl Sandburg married Lilian, or Paula, as he called her, in 1908. She was a highly educated young woman who gave up her career as a teacher to be Carl Sandburg's wife. Later she would apply her intelligence and organizing skills to the raising of an award-winning goat herd.

Chapter 6

Socialism, Love, and Poetry

In 1904, when Sandburg was twenty-six, he confided to Professor Wright that he thought he needed the right woman in his life. "If I could only meet The Ideal Woman, I believe I could pull myself together and set the world by the ears," he wrote in a letter. "As it is, I shall continue to prepare my cocoa myself, sew on the trouser buttons, and be an itinerant salesman, a vagabond philosopher-poet, and a most unworthy descendent of Leif Ericson."[1] Three years later, he would finally meet just such an "Ideal Woman."

Sandburg gave his lecture on Walt Whitman, titled "An American Vagabond," to a large crowd in Manitowoc, Wisconsin, in October 1907. He traced Whitman's career and talked about the chances that the United States would fulfill Whitman's hopes for the country. "If America does not break down before the forces and brutalities that destroyed old civilizations and former republics, it will be because America dares to break away from the traditions that shackle her, it will be because America dreams to experiment," Sandburg said.[2] He was gradually learning how to sell himself, and after his lecture, he wrote a glowing front-page article about the speech in the *Manitowoc Daily Tribune*.

At about this time, political reformers who had founded the Wisconsin Social-Democratic Party were looking for an organizer. The party's leaders were not revolutionaries; they had no intention of overthrowing the government violently. They wanted to reform the government by such measures as taxing wealth, abolishing child labor, and giving women the right to vote. The Socialist movement, although very small, had been growing in recent years. Labor leader Eugene V. Debs ran for president as a socialist in 1900 and 1904, winning small margins of votes but gaining prominence for his ideas and stature as a leader. Socialist leaders in Wisconsin wanted organizers who could educate people about the party's goals and persuade them to join. After hearing Sandburg speak, the organizers thought they had found the perfect person for such a job.

They hired Sandburg and sent him out to the rural areas around Oshkosh, in east-central Wisconsin, to build the party. For Sandburg it was a job in which he could use all his skills as a speaker, writer, and salesman. He wrote articles, gave speeches, and went door to door asking people to join the party and donate money. He could also feel as though he were doing something about aspects of the American political system that had bothered him for years.

One day in December 1907, he stopped by the party offices in Milwaukee to meet with the chairman, Victor Berger. Berger was meeting with a young schoolteacher who belonged to the party and was willing to translate some documents from her native German into English. Her name was Lilian Paula Steichen, and Sandburg was immediately aware that she was the "Ideal Woman" he had written about in his letters and journals. Steichen, a daughter of immigrants, spoke English, French, and German fluently. She was a teacher who had graduated with honors from the University of Chicago. She earned her degree in philosophy in three and a half years, a remarkable achievement even now, but especially so for a woman at the turn of the century. Sandburg asked her to go on a date with him that night, but Steichen declined, saying she already had plans. He asked her for her address, and the two began to exchange letters.

Sandburg sent Steichen some poetry, and she was struck by the quality of his writing. She wrote to tell him that she loved his poems: "The poems— the poems are wonderful! They are different from the poems in the books that stand dusty on my bookshelf—how different!"[3]

Steichen's brother, Edward, had always been artistic. He discovered photography at a young age and would become one of the great photographers of the twentieth century. Lilian Steichen recognized that Sandburg had an artistic genius with words just as her brother had with images. Steichen and Sandburg's affection for each other increased during that winter. As she grew more enamored of him, she invited him to meet her at her parents' farm in Menomonee Falls, Wisconsin, during her spring vacation from school. That week at the farm confirmed what both Steichen and Sandburg already knew in their hearts; they were very, very much in love. They did chores, took walks, and played together in the early spring weather, simply delighted to be in each other's presence.

At the end of the week, they parted sorrowfully. Sandburg went back to his work as a socialist organizer and Steichen back to her teaching job. Sandburg carried pictures of her wherever he went. As soon as he arrived at a new boardinghouse room, he would arrange her pictures on the table and take some comfort from looking at them. "You are with me always as a redeeming, transcending presence," he wrote to her. "The intangible You floats about the room."[4]

By letter, they began planning a summer wedding. They met again at the national convention of the Socialist Party, which was held in May in Chicago. Lilian Steichen shared Sandburg's belief in a new, more just society, and they were both thrilled to be involved in the national conference. Party members, who ranged from poor Oklahoma farmers to New York factory workers, met to write a platform and choose a candidate for the national presidential election in the fall. Eugene V. Debs, who had been a founder of the party and the party's nominee in 1900 and 1904, told the delegates that they should perhaps find a younger person to run for president. After a weekend of lively arguments and spirited debates, the delegates nominated Debs again anyway. Sandburg was elected to the Ways and Means Committee of the national party.

Late into the night, Sandburg worked on what he hoped would be an explanation of socialism that would be easily understood by working people with little formal education. In his article, he posed as an old man in a country village, reviewing what he had learned in years of reading history: ". . . from all that I have studied as to how nations are born and grow and then die, it seems to me that just as soon as a nation gets to the point where a small part of the people are rich and a large part of the people are poor—then that nation is starting to die, the death of it is beginning," Sandburg wrote. "It seems to be a sort of process of slow decay and if you can't stop the process, that nation will go to its grave."[5] Socialist publishers liked the writing in the article, titled "You and Your Job," and republished it widely in magazines and as a pamphlet.

Again, Steichen and Sandburg parted sadly, but by this time they knew they would not be apart for long. They planned to marry in Milwaukee on June 21. Sandburg went back to his organizing work, now with the new goal of lining up support for Debs's presidential bid. Steichen went back to her classroom, where she planned to finish out the year before resigning her job to marry Sandburg. They continued to exchange letters furiously, and Steichen wrote of her hopes for a new kind of marriage based on equality, instead of on a wife's subservience to her husband. "Woman must work with man—think with him—venture with him," she wrote. "Then there's a comradeship and the basis for a deep and lasting love of *souls* as well as bodies."[6]

A week before the planned wedding, Sandburg's sisters, Mary and Esther, came to visit him in Milwaukee, where the state Social-Democratic Party was having its convention. The sisters were astonished to hear that their thirty-year-old, extremely independent brother was engaged to be married a week later, and they liked Steichen immediately. They wanted to return the next week for the wedding, but Mary could not make the trip. At the last minute, Steichen and Sandburg decided to get married that weekend so that both sisters could attend. They took a quick trip to Waukesha to take out a marriage license, and then held a simple ceremony at the home of Carl D. Thompson, a Congregationalist minister and a friend in the Wisconsin Social-Democratic Party. Sandburg and Steichen asked Thompson to remove the word *obey* from the traditional wedding vows, and he agreed.

No sooner was the wedding over than Sandburg was called to aid a friend in trouble. Local business owners had sued Sandburg's friend and fellow socialist Chester Wright, the editor of the *Manitowoc Daily Tribune*, for libel. The business owners said Wright had written damaging lies about their handling of a county fair. Sandburg went to Manitowoc to run the newspaper for Wright during the trial, which ended with the jury finding Wright guilty of criminal libel. After the trial, Sandburg went back to his work as an organizer, fighting the uphill battle to persuade farmers to join the urban workers and intellectuals in the Social-Democratic Party. Lilian was eager to begin a true married life with Sandburg, but during that first summer, Sandburg was too busy working to get Debs elected and building his party to worry about setting up a married household. Lilian was disappointed, but she made the best she could of the situation and waited for his infrequent visits to the farm.

The first time he came to see her, neighbors and friends organized a traditional Midwestern shivaree, a loud serenade that celebrates marriage. Friends blew on horns, shook cowbells, and banged tin cans in a raucous greeting for the newlyweds. They expected Sandburg to treat them all to beer and cigars, but instead he passed the hat to raise money for the Social-Democratic Party. Some donated but others went home, annoyed.

Sandburg campaigned steadily all fall, believing strongly that Debs's victory in the presidential election would make America a better country. The Socialists planned to provide more education and arts opportunities to workers, outlaw child labor, allow women to vote, and institute a progressive income tax so that rich people would pay a higher percentage of their income to support government programs. "We are bent on nothing less than capturing the government for the working class," Sandburg said from a speakers' platform during the campaign.[7] A little over a month before the election, Sandburg boarded Debs's "Red Special" campaign train and traveled with the presidential candidate to Manitowoc, where hundreds of people came to rally for the Socialist Party and hear Debs speak. Sandburg wrote to his wife, telling her how moved he was to meet Debs and hear him speak. "His face & voice are with me yet. A lover of humanity," he wrote. "Such a light as shines from him—and such a fire burns in him—he is of a poet breed, hardened for war."[8]

Debs, in turn, remembered Sandburg fondly. He praised Sandburg's speaking ability and "wholesome presence." Sandburg was "one of the most brilliant young orators in the Socialist movement in the United States," Debs said.[9]

Sandburg's high hopes for victory were dashed on election day. William Howard Taft, popular Republican President Theodore Roosevelt's chosen successor, won the election, with Democrat William Jennings Bryan coming in a close second. Debs was a distant third, polling only 2.8 percent of the popular vote.

Sandburg and his wife rented a few rooms in Appleton, Wisconsin, in the fall of 1908. Carl was still traveling a lot in his work as an organizer, but at last they had their own place and some semblance of a married life. It was a tough winter. The twenty dollars a month Carl made as an organizer was not enough to cover groceries, rent, and heat for their home. During the coldest days, Lilian often went to the library to save money on heating bills. They ate homemade apple butter on homemade whole wheat bread, and little by little Sandburg realized he needed to find a better-paying job.

Sandburg ventured to Milwaukee and began applying for jobs at newspapers. He was an accomplished writer and speaker but had little experience in daily newspapers and could not get hired. Finally Kroeger's, a large department store, hired him to write advertising for its merchandise. Sandburg felt a terrible internal conflict. How could a die-hard socialist go to work for a big capitalist company trying to persuade people to buy things they did not need? He kept at it for a few weeks and got a chance to meet the editors at the city's newspapers. Soon, the *Milwaukee Journal* hired him as a feature writer. Newspaper work was like a salve for Sandburg's energetic, hyperactive personality. He could be everywhere, write about anything, and enjoy the loud, social atmosphere of the newsroom. He began an in-depth investigation of tuberculosis, a bacterial disease also known as consumption that was rampant in American cities at the turn of the century. There was no cure and people with tuberculosis often died young.

After studying tuberculosis, Sandburg came to believe that the disease was in fact a symptom of the plight of the American urban worker. Crowded conditions, overwork, and a lack of sunlight and fresh air made American workers susceptible to tuberculosis, he wrote. Members of the Wisconsin Anti-Tuberculosis Association were so impressed with Sandburg's work that during the fall of 1909 they hired him to travel the state, educating the public about tuberculosis and raising money for the association. Sandburg went on tour with about 200 posters, pictures, and slides, speaking to large audiences eager to know how they could fight tuberculosis. In return for donations, Sandburg sold anti-tuberculosis stamps, known as Christmas seals. Toward the end of the campaign, he was waiting for an overdue train in West Bend with other tired, anxious people, many of them traveling salesmen. Sandburg jumped up and gave his anti-tuberculosis speech with such vigor and enthusiasm that all the salesmen were enthralled and gave generously in return for large numbers of Christmas seals.

With the anti-tuberculosis campaign over, Sandburg returned to Milwaukee in need of a job. He was always writing, and Lilian—who was his expert secretary in those days—sent his articles and poems to various publications. His articles were usually accepted and his poetry was often rejected. The Milwaukee *Social-Democratic Herald* published an article Sandburg wrote celebrating Abraham Lincoln's birthday in February 1910. Sandburg had long written and spoken on Walt Whitman, but the Lincoln article would begin a new obsession for him. Meanwhile, socialists in Milwaukee were organizing for the city election. They had nominated a hardworking, sweet-tempered man named Emil Seidel for mayor, and the possibility of Seidel winning the election filled both Carl and Lilian with excitement. They campaigned arduously for Seidel. Carl spoke, wrote, and went door to door, trying to persuade voters to support him. Lilian went to women's meetings to drum up more support for her candidate.

On Election Day, April 5, 1910, all their hard work paid off. Seidel won the election with 27,508 votes, about 7,000 more than the second-place Democrat earned. Seidel's first appointment was to name Carl Sandburg his private secretary. In the days after the election, Seidel told the city council about his ambitious goals for the city of Milwaukee. He wanted to eradicate child labor, protect the rights of female laborers, improve public transportation, and make the city safer, among many other goals. As Sandburg threw himself into helping Seidel with his large agenda, he began to enjoy some prestige as a writer, speaker, and city official. He bought a new suit and started to become better known. Lilian, who had always wanted to be a farmer, began raising chickens at their small Milwaukee house. That December, Seidel lit the city's first public Christmas tree, which was dedicated to anyone who did not have a Christmas tree to go home to. The Sandburgs loved the tree and were even more enthralled with Lilian's news. She was expecting a child.

As Sandburg exalted in this new life, in which he was for once able to earn a decent living and be home at night, his poetry began to flourish. Lilian gave birth on June 3, 1911, to a daughter whom they named Margaret. Sandburg was thrilled. He wrote a poem titled "Baby Face" in which he celebrated the beauty of the moonlight at the time of his daughter's birth. He wrote, "Keep a little of your beauty / And some of your flimmering silver / For her by the window to-night / Where you come in, White Moon."[10]

Sandburg, who had always enjoyed music, collected songs he heard in his travels. Now that he had a home and a baby, he bought a guitar and began to teach himself a few simple chords so that he could play along with the folk songs he knew and loved. Sandburg had a growing level of confidence in his voice. He composed some unorthodox poetry, such as "I Am the People, the Mob." In that poem he spoke of his belief that working people are at the base of all that is accomplished in the world. "I am the audience that witnesses history. The Napoleons come from me and the Lincolns. They die. And then I send forth more Napoleons and Lincolns."[11]

Seidel and Sandburg were dedicated to making Milwaukee a city that cared for its citizens. However, many of the city's newspapers were against the socialist mayor—the first ever to be elected in a major American city—and they published constant criticisms. Socialist leaders raised money to start their own daily newspaper, and Sandburg became a labor reporter and a columnist at the new paper, the *Milwaukee Leader*. The Republicans and Democrats united in their hatred of Seidel. They formed a new party they called the Nonpartisan Party. Sandburg called it the Nonpartisan Rebunkocrats. They won the election, ousting Sandburg's friend and leaving the poet disenchanted with Milwaukee.

Just as he was growing tired of Milwaukee, a socialist newspaper in Chicago, the *Chicago Evening World*, planned to expand because a newspaper strike had closed all the other papers in the city. Carl, Lilian, and baby Margaret moved to Chicago, eager to start a new life in one of America's leading cities.

After he had moved his family, Sandburg found himself without a job. The *Chicago Evening World* went bankrupt after the strike ended and the other newspapers went back into business. Sandburg walked the streets of the big city, applying for any job he heard about. Finally Negley D. Cochran, the editor of an unusual tabloid called *The Day Book*, hired Sandburg for twenty-five dollars a week. It turned out to be an ideal job for the young poet. Cochran, a political liberal and a careful editor, let Sandburg write about subjects that interested him. He read Sandburg's articles and helped him make his writing extremely clear, concise, and even-handed.

Sandburg fell into a routine of covering labor issues, crime, and city politics for *The Day Book*. At night he'd come home, eat dinner, and then use the stories he had covered during the day to compose poetry about Chicago. He wrote a letter to a friend in which he noted the irony of Chicago—in all its urbanity, ugliness, and greed—as poetic inspiration. "You might at first shot say this is a hell of a place for a poet," he wrote, "but the truth is it is a good place for a poet to get his head knocked when he needs it."[12]

Sandburg liked Cochran, and he liked working for *The Day Book*. But when *System: The Magazine of Business*, offered him a job for thirty-five dollars a week, he accepted. He was embarrassed, as a longtime socialist, to work for an organ of Chicago's business class. He signed his articles with the pseudonym, or pen name, of R. E. Coulson. As Sandburg gradually grew unhappier at *System,* tragedy struck at home. Lilian went into labor with a baby the Sandburgs were going to name Madeline, but the baby died as it was being born. Both parents were devastated by the death. Carl wrote a poem titled "Never Born." It begins: "The time has gone by. / The child is dead. / The child was never even born. / Why go on? / Why so much as begin?"[13]

The death of the baby led to a difficult time for the Sandburgs in Chicago in the fall of 1913. Editors at *System* fired him. Traditional-minded magazines rejected his bold, unusual poetry. In Milwaukee he had been a high-ranking city employee, a popular speaker, a political official. Suddenly he was an unknown, unemployed poet in Chicago. He would find his way back—yet again—through journalism and poetry.

Eugene V. Debs

There is probably no one person in the history of American socialism who accomplished as much as Eugene V. Debs. During his remarkable life, which included two stints in prison and five campaigns for the U.S. presidency, Debs presented the possibility of socialist politics that would free working people everywhere to live decent lives.

Eugene V. Debs

Debs was born on November 5, 1855, in Terre Haute, Indiana. He left school at the age of fourteen to work as a fireman on the railroads. He quickly became involved in what was then a burgeoning movement to unite workers into unions that could win better wages and benefits from corporate owners. In 1880 he was elected grand secretary of the Brotherhood of Locomotive Firemen and as a Democratic Party representative to the Indiana state legislature. He became impatient with both the legislature and the Brotherhood of Locomotive Firemen, which was a narrow craft union open only to railroad firemen.

Debs resigned his union position and founded the American Railway Union with the goal of uniting all the employees of the railroads into one union. The organization grew quickly in 1893, as the Great Northern Railway was lowering workers' wages amidst the Panic of 1893. In 1894, Debs's American Railway Union organized a strike against the Great Northern Railway, and the railroad company agreed to reinstate the workers' wages.

Workers who manufactured Pullman passenger cars also went on strike to protest their declining wages. Debs's union voted to boycott the Pullman cars in Chicago in support of the Pullman strike. The strike interfered with the delivery of the U.S. mail, prompting President Grover Cleveland to order U.S. Marshals and the U.S. military to Chicago to break up the strike. In the ensuing violence, 13 workers were killed and millions of dollars' worth of property was damaged.

Debs and other labor leaders were arrested on charges of interfering with the U.S. mail and sent to prison.

Victor Berger, a Wisconsin socialist, visited Debs in prison and urged him to read Karl Marx's *Das Kapital* and other socialist writings. Debs was convinced that socialism was the answer to the problems of America in the late nineteenth century. When he was released from prison, he became one of the founders of the Social Democratic Party and ran for president in 1900. He ran again on the Socialist Party ticket in 1904 and 1908, all the time campaigning for the rights of workers and women.

Although Debs never won more than a few percentage points at the polls, the ideas put forth by the socialists, such as outlawing child labor and giving women the right to vote, were often adopted by the major political parties, the Democrats and the Republicans. Debs was always known as a great campaigner and a great speaker, but speaking to workers in Utah in 1910, he admitted that he thought workers needed to lead themselves. "I would not lead you into the Promised Land if I could, because if I lead you in, some one else would lead you out. You must use your heads as well as your hands, and get yourself out of your present condition."[14]

The United States was fighting World War I in Europe in 1918, and Debs and other socialists—although not Carl Sandburg—were against American involvement in the war. Debs gave a major antiwar speech on June 16, 1918, in Canton, Ohio. He spoke out against the war and the draft and in support of socialists and pacifists who went to prison rather than fight in Europe. The Espionage Act, a U.S. law, made it a crime to speak against the draft. Debs was arrested and sentenced to ten years in prison, and his citizenship was revoked. At his sentencing hearing, Debs famously said: "Years ago, I recognized my kinship with all living things, and I made up my mind that I was not one bit better than the meanest on earth. . . . While there is a lower class, I am in it, while there is a criminal element, I am of it, and while there is a soul in prison, I am not free."[15]

In 1920, Debs ran for president from prison, with supporters wearing pins that said, "Convict No. 9653 For President." He polled almost a million votes, more than he had received in any previous election. President Warren G. Harding commuted his sentence to time served in 1921, and Debs went home. His health, however, never recovered from his prison time, and he died five years later at the age of seventy.

Sandburg sits at President Abraham Lincoln's old desk, in front of a painting of Lincoln as a young man. Sandburg became an eminent biographer of the beloved president. Even today, decades after it was first published, Sandburg's six-volume Lincoln biography is considered a unique contribution to Lincoln lore.

Chapter 7

Two Books and a War

Carl Sandburg's career as a poet began inching forward during the fall of 1913 and the spring of 1914. Sandburg went to work at *The American Artisan and Hardware Record*, although he could not put his heart into writing articles about different types of tools and hardware for the magazine's audience. Lilian neatly typed some of his poems about Chicago and submitted them to *Poetry* magazine. When the March issue of *Poetry* came out, some readers were aghast at Sandburg's "brutal style." Even so, the publication of the poems placed Sandburg among the city's poets and gave him a new feeling of security. That sense of security was bolstered even more at the magazine's first banquet on March 1, 1914. Carl and Lilian took their seats amid some of the country's best poets, Chicago's leading citizens, university professors, and other artists and benefactors. William Butler Yeats, a great Irish poet, spoke of his vision for poetry, and Sandburg delighted when he heard Yeats call for a poetry that "might exist as the simplest prose."[1] The evening was memorable to both Sandburgs, and especially for Lilian, who had had faith in her husband's poetry even when he did not think it was very good.

After a few uncomfortable weeks at *The American Artisan and Hardware Record*, Sandburg went back to *The Day Book*, where he could write about labor, politics, and the war that was looming in Europe. Europe's governments had seemingly intractable conflicts with one another, and had been steadily building bigger and bigger armies. The spark that lit the fire was the assassination on June 28, 1914, of Austrian Archduke Francis Ferdinand by a Serbian nationalist. Austria declared war on Serbia and asked Germany for support. Serbia called on Russia and France for backing. Germany attacked Belgium, a small northern European country Great Britain had pledged to protect. Great Britain declared war on Germany. Soon millions of soldiers were marching and dying.

Sandburg was horrified as Europe descended into violence. During the day, he wrote newspaper articles about the controversy over whether the United States should take sides in the war. Many in the United States wanted to support France and Great Britain, but others wanted to keep the United States out of the war. In the evenings, Sandburg wrote poetry—at first about his misgivings regarding the war. In one poem, he stands before a bronze memorial of a famous general on horseback and thinks about how war histories always celebrate the politicians and the generals. In "Ready to Kill," he contemplates the idea of a statue that would show a typical working man "feeding people instead of butchering them."

> Then maybe I will stand here
> And look easy at this general of the army holding a flag in the air,
> And riding like hell on horseback
> Ready to kill anybody that gets in his way,
> Ready to run the red blood and slush the bowels of men all over the
> sweet new grass of the prairie.[2]

In the fall of 1914, "Chicago" won the Levinson Prize. Sandburg kept writing, inspired not only by the war in Europe, but also by events at home. In the summer of 1915, about 800 men, women, and children drowned in the Chicago River when the steamship *Eastland* sank. Sandburg was furious at the owners of the steamship and at the government, which had failed to make sure the boat was safe. The tragedy was awful, Sandburg wrote, but bigger, unseen tragedies lurked behind the headlines. Tragedies such as the number of people who die of tuberculosis, the number of babies who die for lack of nutrition, the number of people maimed in railroad work and factory work as their bosses called on them to work faster.

> Yes, the *Eastland* was a dirty bloody job—bah!
>> I see a dozen *Eastlands*
>> Every morning on my way to work
>> And a dozen more going home at night.[3]

Although many of Sandburg's poems were angry—angry about the war, or angry about the government—he also wrote poems about love, joy, and beauty. He walked through Chicago one morning to interview a judge at the courthouse. As he sat in the waiting room, he remembered the way he had just seen the fog come in from the Chicago harbor. He wrote six short lines, simply titled "Fog."

> The fog comes
> on little cat feet.

> It sits looking
> over harbor and city
> on silent haunches
> and then moves on.[4]

In one of Sandburg's angry poems, he denounces a popular evangelist known as Billy Sunday. In the poem, Sandburg said he thought Billy Sunday, who claimed to preach Jesus Christ's biblical message, was really just trying to make money. He used some strong language to say exactly what he thought about the preacher, who was believed to have preached to about 100 million people in 300 revival meetings around the country. Sandburg wrote: "You slimy bunkshooter, you put a smut on every human blossom in reach of your rotten breath belching about hell-fire and hiccupping about this Man who lived a clean life in Galilee . . ."[5] The poem went on for several more lines, each of them dripping with Sandburg's hatred for what he saw as Sunday's fraud and profiteering. Police in New Haven, Connecticut, seized copies of *The New York Call* containing the poem.

Theodore Dreiser, a newspaper writer and a novelist, read many of Sandburg's poems, and he liked them. He suggested Sandburg put together a collection of his poems and offer them to a book publisher. Alice Corbin Henderson, an editor at *Poetry* who had liked Sandburg's poetry since she opened the first package he sent the magazine two years earlier, helped him assemble the manuscript and personally delivered it to Alfred Harcourt at Holt and Company in New York City. Harcourt liked all the poems—even the angry one about preacher Billy Sunday—but he knew other editors at the company would be nervous about the Billy Sunday poem. Harcourt removed the poem from the manuscript, showed the collection to the other editors at the company, and then put the poem back before the book was printed. Meanwhile, Sandburg accepted an offer from his brother-in-law, photographer Edward Steichen, to design the cover of the book.

Holt and Company published *Chicago Poems* in the spring of 1916, and as is the custom in the book publishing world, sent review copies to the major newspapers. Sandburg had been criticized before, but this time, some of the critics seemed to have their knives especially sharpened for him. It was disheartening to see the *Boston Transcript* review, in which Sandburg's work was called a "book of ill-regulated speech that has neither verse or prose rhythms."[6] Other critics were more positive—but perhaps more importantly, regular citizens bought the book and liked the poetry. Louis Untermeyer, a poet who published groundbreaking anthologies, said *Chicago Poems* established Sandburg as the "emotional democrat of American poetry."[7]

There was excitement in Sandburg's home as well. A healthy baby girl—Janet—was born on June 27, 1916.

As Sandburg's career flourished, the drumbeat of war grew louder. Germany threatened to starve Great Britain into submission by attacking even civilian ships carrying food. President Woodrow Wilson, who had promised to keep the United States out of the war, changed his mind. The United States declared war on Germany on April 6, 1917. Many socialists were against the war; they said workers should refuse to kill other workers

Carl Sandburg (left) and Edward Steichen would collaborate on several projects throughout their lives.

for the benefit of capitalists. The U.S. government passed laws making it a crime to harm efforts to recruit soldiers or even to utter disloyal statements about the government or the war. About a thousand people were thrown into prison under the strict new laws, called the Espionage Act and the Sedition Act. Sandburg was in favor of the war, but he did not like to see so many people—including his old friend Eugene V. Debs—go to prison for their political views.

Harriet Monroe called on poets to write about the war and offered a special prize for the best war poem of the year. Sandburg viewed France, Great Britain, Russia, and the United States as four brothers who together would be able to win the war. He wrote "Four Brothers: Notes for War Songs (November 1917)," an epic, five-page poem urging the armies on to victory in Europe. Monroe sent the poem to newspapers across the country, where it was reprinted to wide acclaim. Among many memorable lines, Sandburg wrote, "Look! the four brothers march / And hurl their big shoulders / And swear the job shall be done . . ."[8]

The Day Book, which had long been a comfortable place for Sandburg to work, went out of business in July of 1917. The National Labor Defense Council, which labor unions had organized to support striking workers, asked Sandburg to go to Omaha, Nebraska, to cover a strike. Sandburg stayed in Nebraska for almost a month, and then returned to Chicago and went to work as an editorial writer at the *Chicago Evening American*, a newspaper owned by William Randolph Hearst. Sandburg liked the job, and felt as though his editorials, or opinion articles representing the board of editors of the newspaper, were soundly written. However, Hearst was a well-known conservative, and after a few weeks, Sandburg realized the job was not a good match for him.

Sandburg went to the *Chicago Daily News* and met with managing editor Henry Justin Smith for an hour. Smith hired him as an editorial writer. Sandburg immediately came to like his fellow writers and editors at the *Daily News*, including novelist and playwright Ben Hecht. The Sandburgs compiled a second book of poetry, titling it *Cornhuskers*, and included many of Sandburg's new war poems.

As the war dragged on into 1918, Sandburg decided he wanted to go to Europe. Sam Hughes, the editor in chief of a news service called the Newspaper Enterprise Association, offered him a job as the news service's correspondent for Eastern Europe. Hughes and Sandburg agreed he could be based in Stockholm, the capital of his parents' home country of Sweden, and from there gather news of the war's eastern front. Sandburg was thrilled with the offer and decided to go immediately. The government bureaucracy, however, had other ideas. First of all, Sandburg did not have a birth certificate, so he had to begin by getting his mother to sign an affidavit swearing that he had indeed been born in Galesburg on January 6, 1878. Affidavit in hand, Sandburg went to Washington and New York in July to apply for a passport and buy a ticket for travel to Stockholm. Nothing happened. He found out that the government was suspicious of all non-official travel and was slow and careful about issuing passports. Finally, Sandburg was given a passport at the end of September. He boarded the S.S. *Bergensfjord* to Norway, then took a train to Stockholm. "There was a thrill about seeing the soil of Sweden, setting foot on it, and hearing the speech of one's forefathers spoken by everybody," Sandburg wrote home.[9]

The elation did not last, however. Sandburg sent stories back to Hughes in the United States, but with poor wartime communications, he often didn't know what of his writing was being published. Lilian gave birth to Helga, their third daughter, in November, and Sandburg grew a little lonely and homesick. Meanwhile, he made a big mistake. He unwittingly struck up a friendship with an agent of V.I. Lenin, the new communist ruler of Russia, which had become the Soviet Union. The agent, Michael Borodin, asked him to bring checks for $10,000 to a Finnish organization in the United States. Sandburg checked with the U.S. officials and was told that bringing the money into the United States was not a problem. He packed up lots of pamphlets and books about the revolutionary movements in Europe and Russia and headed for home at the end of December. At U.S. Customs in New York, grim officials detained Sandburg and confiscated his suitcases, questioning him closely about the $10,000 in checks. They suspected Sandburg of breaking a new law, the Trading with the Enemy Act, which prohibits commerce with countries that are considered enemies of the United States. The law carried a possible maximum punishment of ten years in prison. After a week of meetings with intelligence agents, government officials, and prosecutors, Sandburg was released. The officials decided not to charge him with a crime, and he agreed to turn over all the material he had brought home from Europe. It was a frightening, exhausting experience, but Sandburg was comforted by being home again and hearing that *Cornhuskers* received positive reviews. Sandburg is "our Chicago bard, minstrel of our alleys, troubadour of the wheat patches outside our town . . . ," his friend Ben Hecht wrote. "There's more smoke to his song and kick to his heartbeat than Whitman ever coaxed out of his mellow, windbaggy soul."[10]

As the world settled into a short-lived peace, Sandburg was becoming a nationally well-known poet.

World War 1

World War I, or "The War to End all Wars," as President Woodrow Wilson called it, was a devastating four-year ordeal that left about 10 million people dead, empires destroyed, and an uneasy peace that led to World War II. The war not only demolished families and countries throughout the world, but it also had a profound psychological effect. People who had been delighted with the technological advances of the early twentieth century, such as automobiles and airplanes, were horrified to see that modern industrialization could also lead to the invention of new weapons of mass destruction, larger cannons, submarines, tanks, and bomber airplanes. World War I also prompted the first widespread use of poisonous gases on the battlefield.

For about 100 years before World War I, Europe had been fairly peaceful, even though the governments from Germany, France, and Russia mistrusted one another. They developed detailed plans for wars and trained large armies. There were also empires, such as the Ottoman Empire in the Middle East and the Austro-Hungarian Empire in central and Eastern Europe, that dominated large populations of people who were increasingly nationalistic and resentful of imperial control.

Resentment provided the spark that set off World War I. Archduke Francis Ferdinand, heir to the throne of the Austro-Hungarian Empire, traveled to Sarajevo in Serbia. A young nationalistic Serb assassinated Ferdinand on June 28, 1914. His royal family decided to send soldiers to Serbia to reinforce control. They knew that Russia would support Serbia, so they called on Germany for help. Russia attacked Germany. Germany had long secretly planned to attack France through Belgium, instead of through its heavily fortified border with France. When Germany invaded Belgium, Great Britain became involved, because it was committed to protecting Belgian neutrality. The Ottoman Empire in the Middle East supported Germany, so Great Britain sent soldiers to the Middle East to cut off supply routes.

Fighting was fierce for the first few months of 1914. Trenches were dug along battle lines between France and Germany. German soldiers used massive cannons that propelled 2,000-pound bombs. Armies poisoned each other with gases. Great Britain developed tanks. Despite all the blood that was shed and all the people that were killed, a stalemate prevailed for about three years. In 1917, U.S. President Woodrow Wilson overcame American opposition to involvement in the war and began to help with money, technology, and armies. In October 1917, after the successful Bolshevik revolution in Russia, the new leaders withdrew

Russian soldiers from the eastern front.

As the war ended, the violence continued and even spread. More than a million Armenians were killed in genocidal attacks in what is now Turkey. There was a civil war in Finland. Ethnic groups that had long wanted to govern themselves took advantage of the disorder and declared independence. The Czechs and the Slovaks broke off from the Austro-Hungarian Empire and formed Czechoslovakia. Hungarians declared their country independent. New states were also formed in the Middle East.

World War I soldiers wearing gas masks

Leaders of the countries who had won the war—France, Great Britain, the United States, and Italy—met in Paris to plan what they hoped would be a lasting peace. They tried to compromise with Germany, but some leaders insisted that Germany accept responsibility for starting the war and pay debts associated with its cost. The peace agreement, known as the Treaty of Versailles, was supposed to prevent future wars by making sure Germany would never again try to become an imperial power. Some scholars believe that the terms of peace were too hard on Germany. Indeed, economic troubles in Germany after World War I are believed to have helped fascist Adolf Hitler win election in 1933.

Diplomats formed the League of Nations, hoping that such an organization would prevent future wars. The League of Nations had some small successes, but it was powerless to prevent the rise of fascism in Europe, which in just two decades would once again engulf Europe in world war.

Lilian Sandburg typed poetry for Carl when he was starting out. Later she organized their home so that he could work as much as possible and not be distracted. While other famous writers were divorcing their spouses, abusing alcohol, or getting involved in other kinds of destructive behavior, Carl and Lilian Sandburg remained committed to each other and to their family.

Chapter 8

From Newspapers to the National Stage

After returning from Europe, Sandburg continued to work for the Newspaper Enterprise Association, but he gradually fell out of favor with the editors. When he turned in an interview with English playwright John Galsworthy, the editor scolded him for writing about someone who was not well known in the United States. The news service fired him, with apologies, in May 1919, and Sandburg went back to work at the *Daily News*.

Soon after he returned to the paper, Chicago was engulfed in violent riots. An African-American boy was playing at the lakeshore when he drifted into a "whites-only" section of the Chicago public beach. White people there threw rocks at the boy and he drowned. Police refused to arrest the white men responsible for killing the boy. Riots and violence broke out. By the time the violence ended a few days later, 38 people were dead and about 1,000 African-American families were homeless.

Editors at the *Daily News* asked Sandburg to investigate the causes of the riots and write a series of in-depth articles. Sandburg went into the overcrowded, substandard apartments where many blacks lived and asked people to tell their stories. He recorded interviews about the discrimination African Americans suffered, about their poor housing and health care, about the way many of the men had fought tyranny in World War I and returned to find hatred against them at home. "So on one hand we have blind lawless government failing to function through policemen ignorant of Lincoln, the Civil War, the Emancipation Proclamation, and a theory sanctioned and baptized in a storm of red blood," Sandburg wrote in the beginning of the series. "And on the other hand we have a gaunt involuntary poverty from which issues the hoodlum."[1]

The series was published as a book in 1919 called *The Chicago Race Riots*, and again in 1969, when Pulitzer Prize–winning editor Ralph McGill noted that the United States had not paid attention to what Sandburg's series had said back in 1919, and was paying for it with more racial discontent in the 1960s. "This re-issue of Chicago's riot reports . . . is bitter tasting medicine," McGill wrote. "It indicts us as a people addicted to folly and violent resistance to healthful social and political change."[2]

Change of a most frightening kind was coming to the Sandburg home. Their daughter Margaret suddenly began to show signs of epilepsy, an illness of the nervous system that causes seizures in which victims lose control of their bodies and are often temporarily unconscious. The seizures are linked to abnormal electrical activity in the brain. Margaret collapsed into a seizure at school and then again a few days later at home. Both Carl and Lilian were very worried about Margaret's attacks, and they began a long process of seeking out the best possible medical care for her. Epilepsy was not well understood in those days, and there was prejudice and stigma associated with the disease. Carl was earning a decent middle-class income by that time, but he and Lilian realized they would need hundreds, if not thousands, of dollars to take Margaret to the best treatment centers in the country.

Sandburg had always worked diligently, but now he shifted into an even higher gear. He began organizing a series of public appearances in which he would read his poetry and sing folk songs. He had always written his poetry with an eye toward how it would sound when read aloud. When he took to the stage to read his work in his measured, flowing baritone, many audiences were delighted. Emanuel Carnevali, an Italian poet who attended one of Sandburg's first appearances, wrote that Sandburg was a "kingly" reader. "His reading is exactly as beautiful as his poetry and his person," Carnevali stated. "He is one of the most completely, successfully alive human beings I ever saw."[3] Harcourt published Sandburg's third book of poems, *Smoke and Steel*, as he rushed from project to project.

At the *Chicago Daily News*, editors had decided that movies, which had previously been short, comical affairs with little artistic value, were becoming an important new art and entertainment form. When the paper's film critic, W. K. Hollander, went on vacation, the editors asked Sandburg to cover Hollander's beat. Sandburg took over the film critic job permanently after Hollander left the paper. He reviewed hundreds of movies and developed distinct tastes in films. He thought films should be real. If an actor was lost in the wilds of Alaska, his hair should not be perfectly styled. He loved Charlie Chaplin, whose films often satirized modern times. When Sandburg went to Hollywood to interview Chaplin, he surprised the actor as he was getting undressed to take a bath.

Sandburg acted as though such an encounter were perfectly normal, and told his readers: "Before starting for his bath the naked, sinewy, frank, unaffected Charlie Chaplin paused for a short interchange of thought about climate, a warm day's work, and how they had done the same thing over and over fifty times that afternoon."[4] Sandburg knew—especially at the time—that many thought film was not really art. But he thought movies were becoming so pervasive, even in the 1920s, that anyone who did not pay attention to them did not know what was happening in society. "The cold, real, upstanding fact holds—the movies are," Sandburg wrote in 1926. "They come so close to pre-empting some functions hitherto held exclusively by the school and university systems that the philosopher of civilization who doesn't take them into consideration with broad, sympathetic measurement is in danger of being in the place of the drum major of the band who marched up the side street while the band went straight along on the main stem—without leadership."[5]

Sandburg's three lively daughters often asked him to tell them stories. He came up with a make-believe land called Rootabaga and made up stories about its inhabitants. The girls liked the stories, and Sandburg decided to write them down. May Massee, a Chicago children's book editor, helped him organize the stories and look for magazines that would publish them. "They appeal to any age that has imagination and a sense of humor," Massee said to a fellow editor.[6]

Doctors were still trying to help Margaret, and they had figured out that certain foods seemed to contribute to her epileptic attacks. Following a restricted diet seemed to help her avoid seizures. Over Christmas 1921, she went off the diet and gorged herself on some Christmas pastry, which caused some awful seizures. She was confused and dazed afterward, asking her parents if she was going to die.

Sandburg was earning more money from his poetry readings, newspaper work, and royalties on his books. He had a new idea. He asked his publisher, Alfred Harcourt, about writing a biography of Abraham Lincoln specifically aimed at young readers. Harcourt told him the book was a great idea, and Sandburg began working immediately. Now his trips around the country had multiple purposes: interviews with film personalities, performances, and visits to libraries and private homes in pursuit of information about Lincoln. The Lincoln book seemed to take on a life of its own. Books, articles, and pictures filled rooms in the Sandburg home. He rented another room for the overflow and nicknamed it "The Dump."

Sandburg had planned to write a 400-page biography of Lincoln's entire life, but the project kept growing. In 1924, he sent his publisher about 1,000 pages—a massive volume of writing that covered Lincoln's life from birth to his victorious presidential election in 1860. Many books—and many long books—had already been written about Lincoln, but Sandburg brought to it his deep knowledge of American history, dogged, detailed research, and poetic writing style. Lincoln was born, Sandburg wrote, on February 12, 1809, in a dirt-floor log cabin, helped into the world by Aunt Peggy Walters, a local grandmother who served as midwife. "And she and Tom Lincoln and the moaning Nancy Hanks welcomed into a world of battle and blood, of whispering dreams and wistful dust, a new child, a boy."[7]

Harcourt knew he had a potential bestseller in his hands when he received Sandburg's massive manuscript. He decided to try to sell excerpts of the book to a national magazine, something that was often done to promote important books. Virginia Kirkus was then an editorial assistant at *McCall's*, a leading woman's magazine. She stayed up all night reading the manuscript and urged her editor to buy the rights to serialize it. Her editor refused, so Kirkus called a former boss, Helen Walker at the *Pictorial Review*, and told her she should buy the rights. Walker, in turn, stayed up all night with Sandburg's manuscript and became convinced *Pictorial Review* should publish excerpts.

In negotiations with the *Pictorial Review*, Harcourt asked for $27,000 for five 9,000-word excerpts. Sandburg's share would be 80 percent, or $21,600. The magazine editors agreed. Sandburg was lecturing in Texas when he received a shocking telegram from Harcourt:

HAVE SOLD SERIAL RIGHTS LINCOLN . . .
TWENTY–ONE THOUSAND SIX HUNDRED DOLLARS
GET DRUNK AND BE HAPPY.[8]

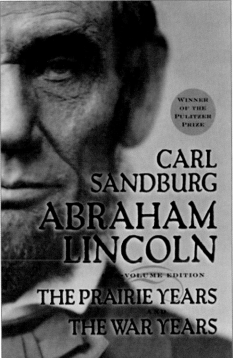

Harcourt published *Abraham Lincoln: The Prairie Years* in 1926 in two volumes, and the book was a huge success. Readers loved the way Sandburg not only portrayed Lincoln intimately, but also revealed with astonishing detail the times in which he lived. "Here is the lining of the old Mid-western mind," wrote one critic. "Here are the songs all people sang, the poems they recited, the proverbs they spoke, the superstitions they could not discard, the machines they used, the clothes they wore. . . ."[9] Malcolm Cowley, a fellow writer, wrote his congratulations to Sandburg: "By God you pulled it off," Cowley said. "Your *Lincoln* is good; it belongs with *Moby Dick* and *Leaves of Grass* and *Huckleberry Finn* . . ."10

Sandburg did not rest on his laurels with the publication of his first Lincoln book. Instead he threw himself into a project that had been germinating in the back of his mind for years. He decided to compile all the old American folk songs he had been noting down on scraps of paper, or learning to play on his guitar, into a big book to be called *The American Songbag*. The book, which Sandburg originally envisioned as a compilation of lyrics without music, became more difficult as he progressed. When he thought he was almost finished, his publisher told him he thought the book should also have each song's music. That idea created months more work for Sandburg as he sought out musicians all over the country who could write down the music for each of the book's more than 200 songs.

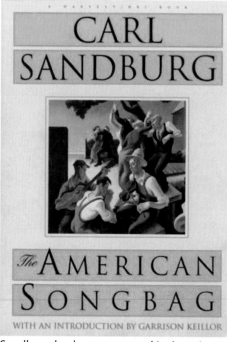

Sandburg broke new ground in American folklore when he compiled *The American Songbag*.

Sandburg had been working for a long time as *The American Songbag* neared completion. Lilian, always the organizer, moved the family to a rented house on Lake Michigan to try to give Carl the space he needed to finish the project. It was there that he collapsed in a nervous breakdown in the summer of 1927. Doctors told him he needed to take a long rest. Lilian took over the work of proofreading pages of *The American Songbag*, while he tried to recuperate by taking long walks and sitting in the sunshine. After a few months, he was ready to go back to work. Finally, in the fall of 1927, *The American Songbag* was released. "The book nearly killed me," Sandburg recalled. "And I am just coming out from under."[11]

Garrison Keillor, who, like Carl Sandburg, would become a great performer and writer, attended a three-room country elementary school in Brooklyn Park, Minnesota, in the 1950s. His teacher owned a copy of *The American Songbag*, and from it, she taught her students songs such as "The Erie Canal" and "I Ride an Old Paint." Keillor loved the book because it was filled with authentic American songs, even the creepy "Hearse Song," with its lines about "the worms crawl in and the worms crawl out."

Later in 1927, Sandburg switched from movie critic for the *Daily News* to a new job as a columnist. In his column, called *Carl Sandburg's Notebook*, he gave his thoughts and opinions on the news of the day. Smith, the paper's editor, was a scholar who believed in hiring great writers and getting out of their way. Donald Russell, a copy editor at the newspaper, remembered that Smith "thought a genius should be let alone. And that was his attitude toward Sandburg."[12]

The 1920s became known as "The Roaring Twenties" because it was a time of prosperity and change. People listened to jazz on their new radios, and they went to the movies as the economy quickly grew. The Sandburgs also prospered and decided to stay on Lake Michigan. With money from Carl's many books and his continued newspaper salary, they built a big, three-story house near Harbert. Times were good for the Sandburgs and the rest of the country, but troubled waters lay ahead.

Abraham Lincoln

The Lincoln Memorial, Washington, D.C.

Abraham Lincoln has become a legendary giant of American history. In his time he was hated and criticized as well as loved and adored as a president who fought to keep the United States together despite an overwhelming conflict.

Lincoln was born on February 12, 1809, near Hodgenville, Kentucky. His mother, Nancy Hanks Lincoln, died when he was nine, and his father married Sarah Bush Johnston. Lincoln grew up on the frontier in Kentucky and later Illinois. He had very little formal education, but he always loved to read. He read the Bible and other books that his beloved stepmother would find for him.

As a young man, Lincoln worked at a general store in New Salem, Illinois. At the store, he developed a reputation as a helpful, friendly, knowledgeable person. That reputation served him well when he ran for a seat on the Illinois legislature. He was elected in 1834 and reelected in 1836, 1838, and 1840. He studied law between sessions and became a Springfield lawyer in 1836.

He became one of Illinois's best-known lawyers as he traveled throughout the state trying civil and criminal cases. The United States, which had been founded just over eighty years earlier on the principal that "all men are created equal," was being drawn deeper and deeper into a conflict over slavery. Large farms throughout the South, known as plantations, used slave labor to grow crops and perform other work. Religious and political leaders were increasingly denouncing slavery on moral grounds. Harriet Beecher Stowe's *Uncle Tom's Cabin* was published in 1852, and thousands of Americans absorbed its antislavery message as they enjoyed the dramatic novel.

The Republican Party of Illinois nominated Abraham Lincoln to run for the U.S. Senate against Stephen A. Douglas. Douglas and Lincoln held seven three-hour debates throughout the state. The debates became famous because of the way Douglas and Lincoln discussed the key issues of the day. Although Lincoln was not elected to the Senate, he gained national prominence as a spokesman for national unity, and was later nominated for the presidency by the Republican Party. In his nomination speech, he said: "A house divided against itself cannot stand.

I believe this government cannot endure, permanently half slave and half free. I do not expect the Union to be dissolved—I do not expect the house to fall—but I do expect it will cease to be divided."[13]

Lincoln was elected in 1860. Southern states began seceding, or breaking away from the Union, before he took office. Lincoln did not want a war, and had long believed in compromises that would lead to the gradual abolition of slavery.

However, the Southern states formed a rebel government known as the Confederacy and attacked a small contingent of federal troops at Fort Sumter on April 12, 1861. The tasks before Lincoln were huge. He needed to raise the money to form and train a large army, manage the existing problems in the government, and find a way to win support for a war that would be long, bloody, and expensive. A meeker man might have shrunk from such an overwhelming task. Lincoln named himself commander in chief, blockaded Southern ports, and suspended habeas corpus, or the right not be held in prison without a good reason.

The first two years of the war went badly for Lincoln, with Union forces repelled at the Battle of Bull Run and at other encounters with the Confederate Army. Lincoln often found his generals too cautious, preferring to wait and withdraw rather than to counterattack and gain territory. Finally, at Gettysburg, Pennsylvania, in July of 1863, the Union forces overwhelmed Confederate troops. In November, as the war continued to go well for the Union armies, Lincoln was asked to make a few remarks at the ceremony to dedicate the Civil War battle-field at Gettysburg. The main speaker, Edward Everett, a well-known orator, spoke for two hours.

Lincoln's speech, on the other hand, was extremely short. In it he said, "The world will little note nor long remember what we say here."[14] And indeed, little note was taken at first. Some newspapers even reported that Lincoln's speech was "silly." *The Chicago Times* said Lincoln "did most foully traduce [degrade] the motives of the men who were slain at Gettysburg" when he said they died "for a new birth of freedom."[15] However, the ten-sentence speech has since gone down in history as one of the best.

Lincoln was reelected president in 1864 as the Civil War drew to a close. He was assassinated shortly after beginning his second term, on April 14, 1865, by a deranged actor named John Wilkes Booth. Lincoln died the next day, and, as Carl Sandburg liked to say, "the Family of Man" mourned a great hero.

Sandburg addressed the House of Representatives, the Senate, the Supreme Court, and President Dwight Eisenhower's cabinet on the 150th anniversary of President Abraham Lincoln's birthday. Lincoln, Sandburg said, is memorialized "in the hearts of lovers of liberty, men and women who understand that wherever there is freedom there have been those who fought, toiled and sacrificed for it."[1]

Chapter 9

A Man of the People

The U.S. stock market collapsed in October 1929, ushering in the Great Depression. People lost their jobs. Farmers lost their farms. The disaster spread across the American landscape. Sandburg had enough money to support his family, but the writer, who had for years mistrusted the way the capitalist economy helped the rich get richer while the poor struggled, was horrified at the toll the Depression took on his beloved country. He wrote of his love and faith for the American people in what became a 286-page poem titled *The People, Yes*. In *The People, Yes*, Sandburg criticized governments, political leaders, and industrial leaders for breaking faith with the hardworking American people. His good friend Oliver Barrett told him *The People, Yes* was too strident in its attacks on the ruling class. Sandburg defended himself, noting that in times of crisis, from the American Revolution to the Civil War, the people who have called for change have often been right. "If Sam Adams, Tom Jefferson and Patrick Henry had kept silence on the exploitation of other American colonists by the imbecile British crown there would have been no American revolution," he told his friend.[2]

After *The People, Yes*, was published, Sandburg returned to his routine of working on the rest of his biography of Abraham Lincoln and traveling the country to sing and lecture. Because of the Great Depression, *The Daily*

News cut all its employees' salaries in half. Sandburg had always enjoyed working at the newspaper, but the salary cut and his desire to spend more time on his Lincoln book prompted him to resign from the newspaper. At home, Lilian and their growing daughters—like families all over the United States during the Great Depression—dedicated themselves to growing food in a big garden. They also bought goats and began producing all the milk, cheese, and butter the family would need.

The family was not immune from tragedy, however. Janet was hit by a car in the fall of 1932 as she crossed the street near the family home. The blow fractured her skull and left her temporarily unconscious. Lilian, who had managed Margaret's epilepsy so skillfully, also cared for Janet as she recovered from her injuries. Helga, meanwhile, remained healthy and became an accomplished horseback rider.

Democratic candidate Franklin Delano Roosevelt was elected in 1932, and he promised a "New Deal" for the American people to restore the country's economy and provide jobs and economic security. Sandburg supported Roosevelt passionately, even as he poured his energy into writing *Abraham Lincoln: The War Years*. After more than a decade, Sandburg finished in the summer of 1939. At times he was discouraged. At one point, he wrote, "Nobody will read it, it's too heavy. . . . My recompense is that I've been on a long journey with one of the greatest companions of men."[3]

Sandburg brought 3,400 typewritten pages to Harcourt in New York. Harcourt's editors, with Sandburg's help, turned the manuscript into a four-volume work of beauty. In those handsome volumes, Sandburg told the story of Abraham Lincoln and the Civil War as it had never before been told. Readers felt as though they were in the telegraph room in the White House when Lincoln received battle news from his generals. And they wept, just as their grandparents had wept at the time, when Sandburg told the story of Lincoln's assassination at the hands of John Wilkes Booth and the massive funeral procession that toured the land after Lincoln's death.

Sandburg traveled to the Rahway, New Jersey, plant where workers printed the book and treated the employees to an evening of poetry and song. He wanted to show them how grateful he was for their work on the multivolume Lincoln biography. The continued slow economy prompted Harcourt to be conservative at first. He ordered 15,000 copies of the set, which would cost twenty dollars each. Even before the printing date, however, orders had come in for 6,000 more copies. Critics, who had so often been divided about Sandburg's other books, were almost unanimous in their appreciation of *Abraham Lincoln: The War Years*. "The poets have always understood Lincoln . . . ," wrote historian Henry Steele Commager. "Sandburg masses his facts in regiments, marches them in and takes the field and the conquest is palpable and complete."[4] *Time* magazine put Sandburg on its cover, and the U.S. literary establishment gave him one of its most prestigious awards, the Pulitzer Prize.

Sandburg's long, exhausting labor ended in triumph, but there was little time to savor the victory. Once again, war was heating up in Europe, and Sandburg was paying close attention. He was convinced that President Franklin Roosevelt was the best man to lead the United States in the looming war. The night before voters would choose between Roosevelt and Wendell Willkie, the Republican Party's nominee, Sandburg spoke on a special live radio broadcast that was heard by 80 million listeners. Sandburg said Roosevelt, like Lincoln, seemed ready to lead the country through the impending crisis. He recalled that the Republican Party was almost unanimously against nominating Lincoln for a second term in 1864, but that a few people gave Lincoln credit for his achievements. One, Reverend Henry Fowler, had said that Lincoln, like Samuel in the Bible, "slowly, and conscientiously and honestly works out the mighty problem."[5]

Roosevelt won the election, and many voters noted the power and beauty of Sandburg's short speech. In December, Roosevelt wrote Sandburg a letter thanking him for his speech. "I have not had a chance since the election to tell you really and truly how much that broadcast of yours closing the 1940 campaign meant to me," Roosevelt wrote.[6]

Sandburg felt a sense of urgency about the frightening political situation in 1940. Fascism seemed to be winning all over the world. Aviator Charles Lindbergh was an American hero after being the first person to fly solo across the Atlantic. Lindbergh, who had lived in Germany, supported Hitler and was against the United States' going to war against Germany. Sandburg attacked Lindbergh harshly and personally during a speech before 24,000 at a pro-war rally at the Chicago Stadium. "The famous flyer who has quit flying and taken to talking doesn't know that the hysteria he mentions is in part the same anxiety, the identical deep fear that men politically free have always had when there were forces on the horizon threatening to take away their political freedom," Sandburg said.[7] As strongly as Sandburg felt about the importance of the fight against fascism, he still had a sense of humor about the ordeal. He and J. Frank Dobie, a Texas professor and writer, had a long history of trading jokes about St. Peter and the gates of heaven. Sandburg joked with Dobie about Nazi propaganda, which was distributed by Hitler's Nazi government and often exaggerated the German army's victories and minimized, or undercounted, any losses or deaths. Sandburg said: "Eight Nazi aviators showed up. St. Pete looked at a memo and said, 'Two of you can come in. The Berlin D.N.B. [the official Nazi news bureau] reported only two of you killed today. Other six will have to go below.'"[8]

Sandburg probably also got a chuckle over an in-depth profile *Reader's Digest* published about him during the war. The *Reader's Digest* writer traveled to Galesburg and interviewed the assistant chief of the fire station where Sandburg had worked while he was studying at Lombard College. The fire chief said he was glad to hear that Sandburg was having success as a writer: "Guess he done right changin' professions. He never was much of a fireman."[9]

In 1943, Sandburg turned sixty-five—an age when many adults consider retiring or at least working a little less. Sandburg, who had achieved fame and fortune as a poet, a biographer, and a performer, turned to an entirely new artistic venture: a novel. He still had friends in the movie industry from his days as a film critic. Two of these men, Voldemar Vetluguin and Sidney Franklin, asked him to write an epic novel of American history that they would then turn into a movie that would uplift the American people and spur them on to victory in World War II.

They asked Sandburg to write the novel in nine months and told him they would pay $100,000. Sandburg signed the contract and eagerly threw himself into the project. He created a character, Orville Brand Windom, who been a justice on the United States Supreme Court. Windom, like Sandburg, loved his country and his history. Shortly before Windom died in the novel, he spoke of his appreciation for the men and women who toiled throughout history to make America the country that it is. "You may bury the bones of men and later dig them up to find they have moldered into a thin white ash that crumbles in your fingers. But their ideas won. Their visions came through. . . . They live in the sense that their dream is on the faces of living men and women today."[10] Windom's heirs find that he has left them a manuscript that brings to life the broad sweep of American history, going back to the American Revolution.

While Sandburg was working on the novel, to be called *Remembrance Rock*, he and Lilian decided to move their family to a farm in North Carolina. Lilian and their daughters were becoming more and more involved with goat farming, and they were tired of the harsh Lake Michigan winters. They found a beautiful farm near Flat Rock, North Carolina. Lilian planned and orchestrated the complicated move, trying to disrupt her husband's work as little as possible. They named the farm Connemara and set Sandburg up in a large workroom with plenty of space for his constantly growing library and boxes and boxes of files. Just as in the Lincoln biography, which grew into six volumes, *Remembrance Rock* became a monstrosity of a novel that Sandburg worked on for four and a half years. He researched thousands of details about 300 years of American history and poured them into the novel, which went on for hundreds and hundreds of pages. He sent boxes of the manuscript to a typist friend in Baltimore and asked her to fearlessly cut out any parts of the book that did not make sense. "It is a butchery business that we are on," he said.[11]

The book was published in 1948, too long after the war to be turned into a pro-war movie, and too long and complicated of a story to be used by Hollywood. The book went straight to the bestseller list and hundreds of readers sent letters to Sandburg thanking him for it. Critics, however, mostly hated the book. *The New York Times* reviewer said it was awful that as good a poet as Sandburg had written such a contrived novel. "There is no more disheartening comment upon our era than to discover that at

Sandburg was best known as a poet and as a biographer of President Abraham Lincoln, but his huge novel of American history, *Remembrance Rock*, was well loved by many fans. His comical Rootabaga stories also entertained children.

this point in his career the author of 'Smoke and Steel' has lent himself to these maudlin devices."[12] Sandburg did not regret anything. He said he had written the type of novel he would have liked to read as a young American, curious about his country and its history.

Remembrance Rock was nominated for a Pulitzer Prize for fiction, but the 1949 award was given to *The Guard of Honor* by Gould Cozzens. As Sandburg neared seventy, his publisher urged him to consider putting out a new, large collection of poems dating back to his beginning. Sandburg joked to a friend, *Washington Post* columnist Thomas L. Stokes, that he was not looking forward to writing a preface for the new collection. "Some 800 odd poems or psalms—or contemplations—for which I must give the world an alibi or thumb my nose at the world and refuse, in so many words, to testify."[13] Despite his joking about needing an "alibi," he wrote a moving preface in which he started out telling stories about baseball, went on to discuss how each person has a different idea about what art really is, and finally confessed that he still worked daily on becoming a writer. "I am still studying verbs and the mystery of how they connect to nouns," Sandburg wrote. "I am more suspicious of adjectives than at any other time in all my born days. . . . I am still traveling, still a seeker."[14]

Franklin Delano Roosevelt

Franklin D. Roosevelt

Franklin Delano Roosevelt was a giant of his time, just the way Abraham Lincoln towered over Civil War history. And Roosevelt, like Lincoln, faced—and overcame—enormous challenges as president.

Roosevelt was born on January 30, 1882, in Hyde Park on the Hudson River in New York State. His parents were wealthy, and Roosevelt enjoyed sports and the outdoors as a child. He went to the Groton School, a prestigious boarding school in Massachusetts, for high school. Afterward he went to Harvard University and then law school at Columbia University.

As a young man he became interested in politics and in the ways that government could be improved and could be used to help society's less fortunate members. He was elected to the New York Senate in 1910. He had married Eleanor Roosevelt, a distant cousin who would become an extraordinarily influential first lady in 1905.

In 1921, he contracted poliomyelitis, a disease that often left its victims paralyzed. Roosevelt, who had always been athletic, tried to recover the use of his legs, but was never able to walk unaided again. His mother urged him to retire from politics, but his wife and a trusted adviser, Louis McHenry Howe, urged him to continue.

Roosevelt was elected governor of New York in 1928. The 1920s had been a time of economic growth. Stock market values constantly increased, so many people bought stocks with borrowed money instead of saving their money in more conservative ways. The continued gambling on the stock market was one of the reasons it collapsed on October 29, 1929. The collapse was devastating and quickly led to a worldwide economic depression. People lost their jobs, ran out of food, and even became homeless as the economy continued to worsen.

President Herbert Hoover, a Republican, could not decide what, if anything, the government should do about the economic collapse. Roosevelt ran for president as a Democrat in 1932, promising to use the government to give the American people a "New Deal." Roosevelt was elected and led the Congress to attack the Depression with vigor during a historic 100 days of legislation that put the government to work at helping people put their lives back together.

Roosevelt created the Work Projects Administration, which gave people jobs repairing roads, building bridges, and improving other public properties. He also created many other government agencies aimed at alleviating the effects of the Depression. He reformed the banking system, providing insurance for depositors and help to homeowners. He also initiated an agency for regulating the stock market called the Securities and Exchange Commission. Roosevelt was a great communicator, holding frequent press conferences and addressing the American people directly in weekly radio speeches known as "fireside chats."

The worldwide economic collapse was one reason that fascism, or the system of government in which a dictator pushes a country to work and produce for military or imperial aims, became popular in Germany, Italy, Japan, and Spain. Fascism was particularly abhorrent in Germany, where dictator Adolf Hitler blamed the country's economic problems on Jewish people. He systemically killed six million Jews and others he considered undesirable. Germany, Japan, and Italy formed a coalition called the Axis powers.

Roosevelt saw the rise of fascism as a threat to the United States, but he knew Americans did not want to fight and die in Europe so soon after sacrificing for European freedom in World War I. He supported Great Britain economically but at first tried to keep the United States out of the war. On December 7, 1941, Japan attacked the United States at the Pearl Harbor naval base in Hawaii, killing about 3,000 Americans and damaging or destroying 200 aircraft, 13 naval ships, and 8 battleships. The United States joined the war against fascism and turned the fight around once again.

Roosevelt organized and promoted a vast program of production to equip the military. He met with the leaders of Great Britain and the Soviet Union to plan strategy, and he spoke eloquently to the American people about the importance of work and sacrifice to win the war. Roosevelt was reelected to an unprecedented fourth term in 1944. However, he did not live to see the Allied victory in World War II. He had a massive stroke on April 12, 1945, just a few months before the surrender of the Axis powers. He was remembered as a groundbreaking president who not only helped win World War II but also supervised the creation of a new kind of American society.

Sandburg and a granddaughter look at one of the goats at Connemara Farm, near Flat Rock, North Carolina, where the Sandburgs lived beginning in 1945. The farm is now a national historic site operated by the U.S. Park Service. It hosts visitors throughout the year and sponsors educational and cultural activities related to the Sandburg legacy.

Chapter 10

Looking Back

Joseph Wershba, a producer for CBS, went to the Sandburgs' farm in December of 1950 to interview Carl for *Hear It Now*, a new CBS radio program. On the way, Wershba's engineer told him that Sandburg was going to insist that Wershba drink goat's milk. The thought made Wershba sick to his stomach. Sure enough, Wershba sat down at Sandburg's house and Carl—who had been drinking goat's milk for years and thought it was delicious and nutritious—immediately offered him a glass of goat's milk. Wershba swallowed his milk as quickly as possible and was grateful that he did not vomit. Trying to be nice, he told Sandburg the milk was "terrific . . . wonderful stuff." He could tell right away that Sandburg knew he was lying. "I knew, don't try to pull the wool over this old buddy's eyes," Wershba said. "He was as sharp as anybody. He knew immediately that I was probably glad that I didn't throw up on the goat's milk."[1]

Goat's milk or no, Sandburg often marveled at his longevity. So many of the writers he liked had died young of alcoholism or illness or suicide. Sandburg, approaching seventy-three, was still fit and capable. He wrote a memoir of his childhood in Galesburg. This time, he did not become obsessed or take years longer than expected. He wrote simply and from his heart about his parents, childhood, and hometown. He told funny stories about boyhood shenanigans such as trying to sneak into the circus, and he wrote poignantly about the death of his two brothers. He recalled his toil in manual labor as a teenager, from distributing newspapers and milk to sweeping floors and shining shoes. The book, titled *Always the Young Strangers*, came out in 1953 and was well loved. "Sandburg here presents ordinary, everyday life in its true simplicity, warmth and dignity," a *Christian Science Monitor* reviewer wrote. "To read him is to share the enduring satisfaction of days well lived, to feel glad you're just common folks."[2]

Sandburg became less outspoken about political matters as he grew older, but he campaigned for Adlai Stevenson, the Democratic Party's choice for president against the Republican Dwight D. Eisenhower in 1952. Stevenson was dear to Sandburg's heart, an outspoken liberal and a former governor of Illinois. Eisenhower was a beloved World War II general. Sandburg accused Eisenhower of having lived off the government all his life and yet saying he was against the socialistic practice of expanding the government. Eisenhower, Sandburg said, "has yet to know the people of the United States. With him the words 'socialist' and 'socialism' are dirty words . . . but ever since he left the creamery at Abilene, Kansas, he never bought a suit of clothes or a meal. . . . He's lived in a welfare state ever since he left Abilene and went to West Point."[3]

Even though Sandburg disliked Eisenhower, he thought a joke that was making the rounds about the president was excessively mean. He nonetheless passed it on to his friend J. Frank Dobie, with whom he planned to one day publish an anthology of jokes about St. Peter and the gates of heaven. Sandburg said the joke had Eisenhower arriving at the gates of hell and Satan tells Eisenhower that he does not belong in hell and should go "up." Eisenhower comes back a few hours later and asks, "Which way is up?"[4]

Sandburg had always kept in touch with his brother-in-law, Edward Steichen, and they had worked together before. Now Steichen asked Sandburg to help him with his masterpiece, an enormous exhibition of photographs collected from around the world and titled *The Family of Man*. Steichen mounted the 503 photographs at New York City's Museum of Modern Art, and Sandburg wrote the introductory text. He celebrated the way the photographs showed that although cultures all over the world may look very different, on a fundamental level, the "Family of Man" is one. "In a seething of saints and sinners, winners and losers, in a womb of superstition, faith, genius, crime, sacrifice, here is the People, the one and only source of armies, navies, work-gangs, the living flowing breath of the history of nations, ever lighted by the reality or illusion of hope."[5] Sandburg concluded his introduction to the exhibit with what would become some of his most famous lines:

> There is only one man in the world
> and his name is All Men.
> There is only one woman in the world
> and her name is All Women.
> There is only one child in the world
> and the child's name is All Children.[6]

In 1959, Sandburg and Steichen, both almost eighty, traveled to Moscow to present *The Family of Man* in the U.S.S.R. It was a huge success, with more than 70,000 people visiting the exhibit on one Sunday. On the way home, Sandburg stopped in Sweden to visit his parents' hometown and receive a gold medal from the king of Sweden. The trip was a triumphant tour for the two old artists and friends.

Sandburg always had a strong sense of solidarity with other writers. Through a friend, he met a young naval officer named Kenneth Dodson in 1945. Dodson had written very descriptive letters to his wife during World War II, and the letters made their way to Sandburg, who quoted them in *Remembrance Rock* and included a character based on Dodson in the novel. After the war, Dodson struggled to become a writer. Sandburg constantly encouraged him and guided him. "You are a man of a thousand stories. Find a framework. Then write it. Then overwrite it and cut it down. Let no day pass without writing it," Sandburg wrote to Dodson. "When the going is good with you, your sentences march and hammer and sing low and what is called style is there in simple perfection. . . ."[7] Dodson worked for years on a great war novel called *Away All Boats*. When it was published in 1954, Dodson said he never would have been able to do it without Sandburg's encouragement.

Sandburg was always being asked to write reviews and blurbs, or short statements of affirmation, for other writers' books. He often had to say no, but when editors from Harper & Brothers asked him to write something about the western poet Thomas Hornsby Ferril's book of poetry, Sandburg wrote, "I have sworn to write no more blurbs but in the case of Ferril I go by the Spanish proverb 'Oaths are but wind.'"[8] He included a glowing review of Ferril's work. He also inspired Langston Hughes, a pioneering African American poet who called Sandburg his "guiding star."

Sandburg's last major project was yet again something completely new. He went to Hollywood to help his friend and favorite filmmaker with a movie about the life of Jesus Christ, called *The Greatest Story Ever Told*. For months, Sandburg met with the staff members on the film, helping them shape the movie and decide on its tone and content. He came back from Hollywood in the winter of 1962, still fit and strong at eighty-four years old. He spent a few days at home and then went to New York City to appear on *The Ed Sullivan Show*.

While in New York, he fell ill with a virus that seemed to sap him of all his strength. Friends in New York cared for him until he could return home. When he did, he found he could no longer work as he once had. Old age had finally caught up with him. That year he mostly stayed at home. He enjoyed visits from old friends and the praise that came with the publication of a book of poems for children, *Wind Song*, and the last book of poetry published while he was alive, *Honey and Salt*. He made it to Washington, D.C., in 1964 to receive a Presidential Medal of Freedom, saluting President Lyndon B. Johnson smartly and saying, "Sixth Illinois Volunteers."[9] All over the United States, but especially in Illinois, schools were being named after the aging and adored poet.

Sandburg was very pleased to accept a "life membership" award given by the National Association for the Advancement of Colored People, or NAACP. NAACP leader Roy Wilkins called Sandburg "a major prophet of Civil Rights in our time."[10]

President Johnson sent him congratulations when he turned eighty-eight in 1966. Sandburg had a heart attack in June of 1967 and gradually grew weak. He died peacefully at home on July 22. He was eighty-nine.

Family members and friends met for a small service at the Wilderness Episcopal Church in Flat Rock a few days later. A minister read Sandburg's poems and the worshipers rang one bell, as Sandburg had suggested in his 1920 poem "Finish."

In September, about six thousand people gathered at the Lincoln Memorial to pay a special tribute to Sandburg. Important literary and political figures sang praises of him. President Johnson read from Sandburg's poem "Money, Politics, Love and Glory." He read:

Who put up that cage?
Who hung it up with bars, doors?
Why do those on the inside want to get out?
Why do those outside want to get in?[11]

Johnson said he mourned Sandburg's death but knew that Sandburg's spirit would live on. "What will live on forever though is his faith—his faith in the individual human beings whom we impersonally call 'Americans,'" Johnson said. "He knew that always in America 'the strong men keep coming on'. . . . I will miss him; we will all miss him. There will not be one like him again."[12]

Sandburg's body was cremated and his ashes were buried under a granite boulder—Remembrance Rock—at Sandburg's boyhood home in Galesburg, Illinois. His brother-in-law and dear friend, Edward Steichen, almost complained about outliving Sandburg. At his ninetieth birthday party, Steichen stamped his cane and said, "I shouldn't be sitting here. Carl should. There are some men who should live forever—Carl was one."[13] But no man lives forever. Everyone dies and leaves a legacy, big or small.

Sandburg's legacy is in his books and poetry, his song and stories. His Flat Rock home has also been turned into a historic site, where visitors can see where he lived and worked and where his wife and daughters raised champion goats. Tourists can experience the barn (where goats are still being raised), see Sandburg's home, and walk the same trails around the land that Sandburg so enjoyed while he was alive. The beauty and tranquillity of the site is a fitting testimony to Sandburg's life.

Edward Steichen

Edward Steichen's long career as an artist, photographer, and patriot led him from the fashion magazines of Manhattan to the battlefields of both world wars. Steichen was a tireless believer in the power of images.

Steichen was born in the small European country of Luxembourg in 1881. His parents were both poor, so Steichen's father, Jean Pierre Steichen, packed the family's heirloom linens and tablecloths into a few trunks and sailed to America to try to make a better life. He planned to send for his wife and son when he had found a job. However, the father could not find work in America, and after a frustrating time finally gave up and consigned himself to living in an inexpensive boardinghouse. He gradually sold the family's fine linens to pay for food. His wife grew worried when she did not hear from him and, taking Edward, traveled to New York by ship to look for her husband. After weeks of searching in New York, she guessed he might have gone to Chicago. She and Edward traveled to that city to continue the search. There she found him, and upon seeing her and their son, Jean Pierre Steichen regained his will to live. They moved to Hancock, Michigan, after hearing that work was available in the copper mines there. Lilian Steichen was born when Edward was four years old.

Edward went to a college preparatory school near Milwaukee and studied painting. As a boy, he sold newspapers and vegetables from the family's garden. He used the money to buy one of Eastman Kodak's new inventions: a camera. Only one of the first forty-nine frames of film Steichen took had an image on it, but he was nonetheless fascinated. As a young man he worked as an apprentice in a lithographic firm, painted pictures, and continued to study photography. In 1899, Edward moved to Europe to work and study art and photography. He quickly became a boy wonder in Paris, France. He married Clara Smith and the family established a second home in New York.

Steichen became a famous photographer who took pictures of celebrities for fashion magazines and of presidents for news magazines. During World War I and World War II, he volunteered to work as a photographer for the U.S. military. He supervised teams of photographers in Europe during World War I and in the Pacific theater during World War II.

When Steichen retired from photography, he dedicated himself to breeding flowers at his home in Connecticut. He died in 1973, at the age of ninety-four. His art, however, remained prestigious. A picture he took

Edward Steichen's self-porttrait, 1901

in 1904, called *The Pond-Moonlight*, broke a record for photograph prices when it brought $2.9 million at an auction on February 15, 2006.

Although Steichen's art made him wealthy, Sandburg said he was first and foremost a patriot. "Toils, hardships, and dangers are little or nothing to him alongside the American dream," Sandburg wrote. "He is no particular hand at patriotic speeches but he has some mystic concept of the country and its flag."[14]

Chronology

1878	Born in Galesburg, Illinois, to Swedish immigrant parents on January 6
1892	Mourns the death—of diphtheria—of two younger brothers, Emil and Fred
1893	Sister Martha Clara is born
1897	Wanders west as a hobo
1898	Serves in Puerto Rico in the Spanish-American War; fails grammar and math exams at West Point; enrolls at Lombard College
1903	Leaves Lombard College without earning a degree
1907	Goes to work as a Socialist party organizer in Wisconsin
1908	Marries Lilian Steichen
1909	Works for the Wisconsin Anti-Tuberculosis Association
1910	Serves as secretary for Milwaukee Mayor Emil Seidel; father dies
1911	Delights in the birth of his first daughter, Margaret, on June 3
1912	Moves to Chicago; works at *The Day Book*
1914	Wins the Levinson Prize for the best American poem
1916	Daughter Janet is born on June 27
1918	Travels to Europe to write about World War I; daughter Helga is born on November 15
1919	Investigates the Chicago Race Riots for the *Chicago Daily News*
1920	Becomes a film critic for the *Daily News*; publishes *Smoke and Steel*
1924	Finishes first part of six-volume Abraham Lincoln biography
1927	Publishes *American Songbag*
1929	Resigns from the *Daily News* to work full-time on the rest of his Lincoln biography
1936	*The People, Yes* is published
1940	Wins the Pulitzer Prize for History with *Abraham Lincoln: The War Years*
1942	Writes column for the *Chicago Times*
1948	*Remembrance Rock* is published
1951	Wins the Pulitzer Prize for Poetry with *Complete Poems*

1952	Receives the American Academy of Arts and Letters Gold Medal for history and biography
1954	Publishes one-volume edition of Lincoln biography, *Abraham Lincoln: The Prairie Years and the War Years*
1956	The University of Illinois pays $30,000 for Sandburg's library and papers
1959	Becomes the first private citizen ever to address both houses of the U.S. Congress
1960	Works in Hollywood on the movie *The Greatest Story Ever Told*
1962	Is designated "poet laureate of Illinois"
1967	Is awarded the Presidential Medal of Freedom by President Lyndon B. Johnson
1967	Dies on July 22 at the age of eighty-nine

Selected Works

Abraham Lincoln: The Prairie Years and the War Years

Always the Young Strangers

American Songbag

The Chicago Race Riots

The Complete Poems of Carl Sandburg

Home Front Memo

The Letters of Carl Sandburg

"The Movies Are:" Carl Sandburg's Film Reviews and Essays, 1920–1928

The People, Yes

Poems for Children Nowhere Near Old Enough to Vote

Prairie-Town Boy

Rootabaga Stories

The Sandburg Range

Timeline in History

1831	Slaves led by Nat Turner rebel in Virginia.
1844	Samuel Morse sends the first telegraph message from Washington to Baltimore.
1846	The United States goes to war against Mexico.
1849	About 80,000 people flock to California looking for gold.
1850	Under Senator Henry Clay's compromise, California becomes a non-slave state and New Mexico and Utah are admitted without a decision on slavery.
1852	Harriet Beecher Stowe publishes *Uncle Tom's Cabin*.
1854	Political activists opposed to the Kansas-Nebraska Act, which allows settlers in those states to decide on slavery, start the Republican Party.
1858	Abraham Lincoln debates Senator Stephen A. Douglas across Illinois.
1860	Abraham Lincoln is elected president.
1861	The Civil War begins.
1865	The Civil War ends with the Confederacy surrendering, and Lincoln is assassinated.
1885	Chicago developers build the first skyscraper.
1898	The Spanish-American War is fought.
1903	Orville and Wilbur Wright fly the first controlled, powered airplane.
1909	The National Association for the Advancement of Colored People is founded.
1915	The steamship *Eastland* sinks near Chicago, killing about 800 passengers.

1917	The United States joins World War I.
1918	World War I ends.
1929	The stock market crash ushers in the Great Depression.
1941	The United States joins World War II.
1945	World War II ends.
1955	Rosa Parks refuses to get off a bus in Montgomery, Alabama, beginning the civil rights movement.
1963	President John F. Kennedy is assassinated.
1964	The U.S. Congress passes the Gulf of Tonkin resolution, giving President Lyndon B. Johnson permission to wage war in Vietnam.
1975	United States forces leave Vietnam, and the North Vietnamese troops take power in Saigon.
1980	The United States boycotts the Olympics to protest the Soviet Union's invasion of Afghanistan.
1995	International terrorists bomb Oklahoma City, killing 168 people.
2001	Terrorists attack the United States, crashing airplanes into the World Trade Center, the Pentagon, and a field in Pennsylvania.
2006	President George W. Bush's popularity plunges to an all-time low as violence continues in Iraq, three years after Bush ordered the invasion of that country.

Chapter Notes

Chapter 1
A Shock in Chicago

1. Carl Sandburg, *The Complete Poems of Carl Sandburg* (New York: Harcourt Brace Jovanovich, 1969), pp. 3–4.

2. Penelope Niven, *Carl Sandburg: A Biography* (New York: Charles Scribner's Sons, 1991), p. 243.

3. Ibid., p. 252.

4. Ibid., p. 253.

5. About *Poetry*, **http://www. poetrymagazine.org/about/**

6. Ezra Pound, "To Whistler, American," **http://www. poetrymagazine.org/magazine/ 1210/1210_pound2.html**

7. Joyce Kilmer, "Trees," **http:// www.bartleby.com/104/119.html**

8. Niven, p. 237.

Chapter 2
A Child of Immigrants

1. Carl Sandburg, *Always the Young Strangers* (New York: Harcourt Brace Jovanovich, 1953), p. 20.

2. Ibid., p. 112.

3. Ibid., p. 99.

4. Ibid., pp. 187–188.

5. Ibid., p. 61.

6. Ibid., p. 64.

7. Carl Sandburg, *Abraham Lincoln: The Prairie Years and the War Years* (New York: Harcourt, 1954), p. 445.

8. Sandburg, *Always the Young Strangers*, p. 218.

9. Ibid., p. 207.

10. Ibid., p. 208.

11. Kathleen Krull, *I Hear America Singing* (New York: Knopf, 2003), p. 18.

Chapter 3
A Teenager in Hard Times

1. Carl Sandburg, *Always the Young Strangers* (New York: Harcourt Brace Jovanovich, 1953), p. 92.

2. Ibid., p. 222.

3. Ibid., p. 223.

4. Penelope Niven, *Carl Sandburg: A Biography* (New York: Charles Scribner's Sons, 1991), p. 20

5. Sandburg, p. 245.

6. Ibid., p. 254.

7. Ibid., p. 227.

8. Ibid., p. 246.

9. Ibid., p. 377.

10. Ibid., p. 184.

Chapter 4
A Hobo and a Soldier

1. Carl Sandburg, *Always the Young Strangers* (New York: Harcourt Brace Jovanovich, 1953), p. 385.

2. Ibid., p. 390.

3. Ibid., p. 397.

4. Ibid., p. 391.

5. Ibid, p. 405.

6. William Knox, "Oh, Why Should the Spirit of Mortal Be Proud?" on "Abe Lincoln, Poet," **http://people.whitman.edu/ ~hashimiy/abe.htm**

7. Sandburg, p. 414.

8. Ibid., p. 419.

9. Library of Congress, Mark Twain 1835–1919, **http://www.loc. gov/rr/hispanic/1898/twain.html**

Chapter 5
A Restless Young Man

1. Penelope Niven, *Carl Sandburg: A Biography* (New York: Charles Scribner's Sons, 1991), p. 52.

2. Ibid., p. 55.

3. Ibid., p. 63.

4. Ibid., p. 85.

5. Ibid., p. 67.

6. Walt Whitman, *Leaves of Grass* (New Jersey: Replica Books, 2002), p. 379.

Chapter 6
Socialism, Love, and Poetry

1. Penelope Niven, *Carl Sandburg: A Biography* (New York: Charles Scribner's Sons, 1991), p. 90.

2. Ibid., p. 133.

3. Ibid., p. 151.

4. Ibid., p. 158.

5. Ibid., p. 169.

6. Ibid., p. 177.

7. Ibid., p. 187.

8. Ibid., p. 193.

9. Ibid., p. 197.

10. Carl Sandburg, *The Complete Poems of Carl Sandburg* (New York: Harcourt Brace Jovanovich, 1969), p. 131.

11. Ibid., p. 71.

12. Niven, p. 231.

13. Sandburg, p. 265.

14. Nick Salvatore, *Eugene V. Debs: Citizen and Socialist* (Champaign: University of Illinois), p. 229–230.

15. David Zirin, "The Fight to Save Stanley Tookie Williams," **http://www.thenation.com/ doc/20051212/zirin**

Chapter 7
Two Books and a War

1. Penelope Niven, *Carl Sandburg: A Biography* (New York: Charles Scribner's Sons, 1991), p. 240.

2. Carl Sandburg, *The Complete Poems of Carl Sandburg* (New York: Harcourt Brace Jovanovich, 1969), pp. 28–29.

3. Niven, p. 264.

4. Sandburg, p. 33.

5. Niven, p. 265.

6. Ibid., p. 276.

7. Ibid., p. 281.

8. Sandburg, p. 147.

9. Niven, p. 315.

10. Ibid., p. 335.

5. Carl Sandburg, *The Movies Are* (Chicago: Lake Claremont Press, 2000), preface (unpaged).

6. Niven, p. 384.

7. Carl Sandburg, *Abraham Lincoln: The Prairie Years and the War Years* (New York: Harcourt Inc., 1954), p. 7.

8. Niven, p. 426.

9. Ibid., p. 434.

10. Ibid., p. 437.

11. Ibid., p. 463.

12. Ibid., p. 456.

13. Carl Sandburg, *Abraham Lincoln: The Prairie Years and the War Years*, p. 138.

14. Ibid., p. 444.

15. Ibid., p. 445.

Chapter 8
From Newspapers to the National Stage

1. Carl Sandburg, *The Chicago Race Riots: July, 1919* (New York: Harcourt, Brace and Howe, 1919), p. 4.

2. Ibid., p. xvii.

3. Penelope Niven, *Carl Sandburg: A Biography* (New York: Charles Scribner's Sons, 1991), p. 348.

4. Ibid., p. 375.

Chapter 9
A Man of the People

1. Penelope Niven, *Carl Sandburg: A Biography* (New York: Charles Scribner's Sons, 1991), p. 680.

2. Ibid., p. 502.

3. Ibid., p. 496.

4. Ibid., p. 534.

5. Carl Sandburg, *Home Front Memo* (New York: Harcourt, Brace and Company, 1943), p. 30.

6. Niven, p. 539.

7. Ibid., p. 546.

8. Herbert Mitgang, editor, *The Letters of Carl Sandburg* (New York: Harcourt, Brace & World, 1968), p. 391.

9. Niven, p. 545.

10. Carl Sandburg, *Remembrance Rock* (New York:Harcourt, Brace and Company, Inc., 1948), p. 21.

11. Niven, p. 585.

12. Ibid., p. 589.

13. Mitgang, p. 466.

14. Carl Sandburg, *The Complete Poems of Carl Sandburg* (New York: Harcourt Brace Jovanovich, 1969), p. xxxi.

Chapter 10
Looking Back

1. Penelope Niven, *Carl Sandburg: A Biography* (New York: Charles Scribner's Sons, 1991), p. 603.

2. Horace Reynolds, "A Picture of a Town and Its People," *Christian Science Monitor*, January 8, 1953, p. 11.

3. Niven, p. 689.

4. Herbert Mitgang, editor, *The Letters of Carl Sandburg* (New York: Harcourt, Brace & World, 1968), p. 500.

5. Edward Steichen, *The Family of Man* (New York: The Museum of Modern Art, 1955), prologue by Carl Sandburg (unpaged).

6. Ibid.

7. Niven, p. 592.

8. Mitgang, p. 481.

9. Niven, p. 696.

10. Niven, p. 699.

11. Carl Sandburg, *The Complete Poems of Carl Sandburg* (New York: Harcourt Brace Jovanovich, 1969), p. 394.

12. Lyndon B. Johnson, "Remarks at the Memorial Service for Carl Sandburg, September 17, 1967" (Washington, D.C.: Government Printing Office, Federal Register Division, National Archives and Records Service), pp. 841–842.

13. Helga Sandburg, *A Great and Glorious Romance: The Story of Carl Sandburg and Lilian Steichen* (New York: Harcourt, Brace & Jovanovich, 1978), p. 314.

14. Niven, p. 684.

Further Reading

For Young Adults

Franchere, Ruth. *Carl Sandburg: Voice of the People*. Champaign, Illinois: Garrard Publishing Company, 1970.

Meltzer, Milton. *Carl Sandburg: A Biography*. Minneapolis: Millbrook Press, 1999.

Mitchell, Barbara. *Good Morning, Mr. President: A Story About Carl Sandburg*. Minneapolis: Carolrhoda books, 1988.

Niven, Penelope. *Carl Sandburg: Adventures of a Poet*. New York: Harcourt Inc., 2003.

Works Consulted

D'Allessio, Gregory. *Old Troubadour*. New York: Walker and Company, 1987.

Golden, Harry. *Carl Sandburg*. Cleveland: The World Publishing Company, 1961.

Johnson, Lyndon B. "Remarks at the Memorial Service for Carl Sandburg, September 17, 1967." Washington, D.C.: Government Printing Office, Federal Register Division, National Archives and Records Service.

Krull, Kathleen. *I Hear America Singing*. New York: Knopf, 2003.

Mitgang, Herbert, editor. *The Letters of Carl Sandburg*. New York: Harcourt, Brace & World, 1968.

Niven, Penelope. *Carl Sandburg: A Biography*. New York: Charles Scribner's Sons, 1991.

Reynolds, Horace. "A Picture of a Town and Its People." *Christian Science Monitor*, January 8, 1953.

Sandburg, Carl. *Abraham Lincoln: The Prairie Years and the War Years*. New York: Harcourt Inc., 1954.

_____. *Always the Young Strangers*. New York: Harcourt Brace Jovanovich Publishers, 1953.

_____. *The Chicago Race Riots*. New York: Harcourt, Brace and Howe, 1919.

_____. *The Complete Poems of Carl Sandburg*. New York: Harcourt, 1970.

_____. *Home Front Memo*. New York: Harcourt, Brace and Company, 1943.

_____. *The Letters of Carl Sandburg*. New York: Harcourt, Brace & World, Inc., 1968.

_____. "The Movies Are": Carl Sandburg's Reviews and Essays, 1920–1928.
  Chicago: Lake Claremont Press, 2000.

_____. Remembrance Rock. New York: Harcourt, Brace and Company, 1948.

Sandburg, Helga. A Great and Glorious Romance: The Story of Carl Sandburg
  and Lilian Steichen. New York: Harcourt Brace Jovanovich, 1978.

Steichen, Edward. The Family of Man. New York: The Museum of Modern Art,
  1955.

Whitman, Walt. Leaves of Grass. New Jersey: Replica Books, 2002.

On the Internet

The Carl Sandburg Historic Site, Galesburg, Illinois
http://www.sandburg.org

Library of Congress, *Mark Twain*, 1835–1919
http://www.loc.gov/rr/hispanic/1898/twain.html

National Park Service: Carl Sandburg Home
http://www.nps.gov/carl/index.htm

Poetry Magazine
http://www.poetrymagazine.org

Reynolds, Stephen Marion. "Life of Eugene V. Debs"
http://www.marxists.org/archive/debs/bio/bio.htm

Van Wienen, Mark W. *Modern American Poetry: Carl Sandburg*
www.english.uiuc.edu/maps/poets/s_z/sandburg/sandburg.htm

Glossary

alibi (AA-lih-bye) A statement of being in a different place when a crime was committed.

asphalt (AS-fallt) A black by-product of petroleum production that contains hydrocarbons.

atrocity (ah-TRAH-sih-tee) An act of extreme violence or cruelty.

baritone (BAA-rih-tohn) Intermediate male voice between a tenor and a bass.

blasphemous (BLAS-fuh-mus) Sacrilegious or profane.

cornea (KOR-nee-ah) A transparent membrane the covers the eye.

draft Selection for obligatory military service.

fascism (FAA-shism) A political belief system that holds a certain country above others and controls political and economic activity, usually with militaristic aims.

free verse Poetry that does not follow a system of rhyming words or number of syllables in each line.

gold standard A monetary system during the nineteenth century in which money had fixed value and could be exchanged for gold in the government's treasury.

libel (LYE-bul) The purposeful written publication of information that is false and damaging.

maudlin (MAWD-lin) Weakly sentimental.

populist (PAH-pyoo-list) A member of a political party that claims to represent the common folk.

shenanigans (sheh-NAA-nih-ghins) Foolish behavior; trickery.

solidarity (sah-lih-DAYR-ih-tee) The concept of unity with others for a common purpose or goal.

striker (STRYE-ker) A person who walks off a job in unity with other employees to pressure an employer for better wages and /or benefits.

subservience (sub-SUR-vee-ans) A position of being below or subordinate to someone else.

unorthodox (un-OR-thuh-doks) Not in agreement with ordinary conventions.

Index